From Reviews of Eric Maisel's Previous Books

"Eric Maisel has made a career out of helping artists, musicians, dancers, and writers cope with the traumas and troubles that are the price of admission to a creative life." — *Intuition* magazine

"Eric Maisel has fused his empirical knowledge of the artistic life with true empathy and support for artists in each of the disciplines." — *New Age Journal*

Praise for *Brainstorm* by Eric Maisel and Ann Maisel

"[*Brainstorm*] is a book that should be read by all who want to live their life in a way that is vital and leaves some kind of legacy. It's not about fame and fortune, but rather, about ensuring that this brief span that we have on Earth is one that has value — where we leave some kind of impression. There's nothing that matters more." — *Seattle Post-Intelligencer*

"All too often people overlook the basics of a productive life, distracted by multitasking, marketing, and information overload. With this provocative departure from the usual lifestyle manual, the Maisels are out to break us of those tendencies." — *Publishers Weekly*

"Presents a new way of thinking about how to turn brain potential into passion, energy, and genuine accomplishments." — Camille Minichino, physicist and author of the Periodic Table Mysteries

"What a pivotal way to experience your brain and all that it can create! I love that this book celebrates and teaches the concept of productive obsession and the multitudinous gifts of brainstorming." — SARK, artist and author of *Glad No Matter What* and other books (www.PlanetSARK.com)

Praise for *Rethinking Depression* by Eric Maisel

"In this riveting deconstruction of the 'mental health industry,' Eric Maisel provides essential tools to address human despair. Although it will provoke controversy, *Rethinking Depression* is one of the most perceptive and accessible guides to life fulfillment that I have ever read." — Kirk Schneider, PhD, author of *Existential-Humanistic Therapy* and *Awakening to Awe*

"*Rethinking Depression* is an important and timely book that busts numerous myths about why people have the so-called mental illness of 'depression.' Eric Maisel gives readers a path and a language that will help them shine a light on the dark side of unhappiness and move toward a meaningful, self-directed life."
— Richard Bargdill, membership chair and executive board member, Society for Humanistic Psychology

"An uplifting and practical guide to life and how to live it better. Eric Maisel has made existential thinking accessible to all those who want to live their lives in a more deliberate and engaged fashion."
— Emmy van Deurzen, principal, New School of Psychotherapy and Counseling, London, and author of *Psychotherapy and the Quest for Happiness*

Praise for Eric Maisel's Creativity Coaching

"Without Eric Maisel's guidance I would never have successfully negotiated the publishing process. With his help, I completed a substantial proposal, landed a good agent, and just saw my first book published!"
— Nancy Pine, author of *Educating Young Giants*

"It's been an unexpected joy to find someone as creatively supportive and encouraging as Eric Maisel. I didn't know what to expect out of our sessions, and each one is fresh and interesting. Eric is inspirational!"
— Christine Collister, international recording artist

"Eric Maisel's insights have helped me with every aspect of my painting career, from the evolution of my market vision to strategies for self-promotion. I also found his help invaluable in feeding my creator's soul!"
— Jonathan Herbert, painter and photographer

"I began my novel in one of Eric Maisel's Deep Writing workshops, finished it in another, and quickly sold it for a lovely advance. Eric, his individual coaching, and his writing workshops have made all the difference in my writing life."
— Eva Weaver, author of *The Puppet Boy of Warsaw*

"I'm an executive coach and the author of two books, and Eric Maisel is my coach. No one is better qualified to lead a creative person on his or her creative journey."
— Jackee Holder, author of *Be Your Own Best Life Coach*

MAKING YOUR CREATIVE MARK

ALSO BY ERIC MAISEL

MAKING YOUR CREATIVE MARK

NINE KEYS TO ACHIEVING YOUR ARTISTIC GOALS

ERIC MAISEL

New World Library
Novato, California

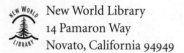

New World Library
14 Pamaron Way
Novato, California 94949

Text design by Tona Pearce Myers

Library of Congress Cataloging-in-Publication Data
Maisel, Eric, date.
Making your creative mark : nine keys to achieving your creative goals / Eric Maisel.
     pages cm
Includes index.
ISBN 978-1-60868-162-4 (pbk. : alk. paper) — ISBN 978-1-60868-163-1 (ebook)
1. Creation (Literary, artistic, etc.) 2. Creative ability. 3. Arts—Psychological aspects. 4. Artist's block. 5. Artists—Psychology. I. Title.
BF408.M2325 2013
53.3'5—dc23   2012049576

First printing, April 2013
ISBN 978-1-60868-162-4
Printed in Canada on 100% postconsumer-waste recycled paper

New World Library is proud to be a Gold Certified Environmentally Responsible Publisher. Publisher certification awarded by Green Press Initiative. www.greenpressinitiative.org

10 9 8 7 6 5 4 3 2 1

For Tiffany —
so glad you're part of the family!

For the artists everywhere with whom I've worked.

And, as always, for Ann.

CONTENTS

INTRODUCTION

've been working with creative and performing artists and other creative types — businesspeople, scientists, academics, lawyers, physicians, and folks from all different callings — for the past thirty years.

I've worked with MacArthur fellows, bestselling authors, and Academy Award winners; with teenagers who are just starting out; with unrecognized painters, writers, and musicians who bring love and commitment to each new project, despite their lack of marketplace success; with creators in every conceivable set of circumstances.

I've worked with rooms full of British artists, German artists, Flemish artists, and I've facilitated workshops in small towns and in cities such as Paris, London, Berlin, and New York. Thousands of creative and performing artists have come forward to be coached for free by the creativity coaches that I train — and each of these thousands of artists has told me his or her story.

Many aspects of my coaching and teaching practice have changed over the years. Not so long ago I always traveled somewhere to do a workshop. Today I'm just as likely to visit virtually or via telechats. For instance, in September of this year I'll present the keynote address at a creativity conference in Bogotá, Colombia — via Skype, while sitting at my desk at home. The next day I'll lead a workshop for thirty Colombian participants — again, virtually.

These changes are natural and even inevitable as technology makes them possible, and as I get older and busier. What does not change are the problems. The human beings who come to me want to create or perform. Most not only want to create or perform but also hope to do good work that is desired and respected. So much stands in the way of their realizing their dreams, goals, and ambitions! So much that I have written book after book exploring the answer to *this* problem and the answer to *that* problem and the answer to the *next* problem.

In short, I've seen a lot and I've written a lot, more than twenty books' worth, about artists and depression, artists and anxiety, artists and addiction — analyzing the issues of the creative personality and the creative life. In this book I want to distill those lessons and identify what it takes to achieve your best possible life in the arts. In short, I hope to provide you with a user's manual for your creative journey.

Each of the nine issues I describe in this book is of vital importance to anyone who creates or wants to create. Most likely you know how often you stall, block, and give up. Most likely you understand that the art marketplace is a difficult place. Most likely you understand how often time gets away from you, how often you fret about whether what you're attempting matters to anyone, including yourself, and how often your discipline eludes you. You can name the challenges.

But what to do about them? Mastering the nine keys in this book will help you tremendously.

What's stopping you may be a lack of internal freedom — to speak up, to make messes, to have a point of view. It may be that stress is stopping you in your tracks. It may be that you don't know how to get a grip on your mind and prevent yourself from thinking thoughts that don't serve you. It may be that you lack confidence, that you have trouble kindling your passion, or that you communicate poorly in the marketplace. We will look at all those issues.

I hope that the following discussions will help you clarify what it takes to create regularly and deeply and to negotiate the challenges of the creative life. If you were suddenly handed enough time and all the energy in the world, you would still have to master these nine challenges in order to get your creating done. I hope this book presents you with a clear picture of these challenges — and points you to the solutions.

What do I mean by "your best life in the arts"? I see it as the following. You get to create or perform — that is, you get to do the thing you love to do. You have at least some successes. You avoid as many pitfalls as possible, including those that you put in your own way by virtue of your personality shadows. You create a life that includes creating but is not limited to creating: you make meaning in many different ways. You make yourself proud by your efforts, and you grab a slice of the art marketplace pie. All that is something.

You may well be wishing for more. You may be wishing for bestsellers, eye-popping fame, and huge paydays. Yes, these things are certainly pretty to think about! I am not against any of them. However, your best life in the arts, even if it doesn't include stardom and huge piles of money, may still be a beautiful and rewarding thing.

Life is, after all, not a question with an answer — it is a project to be lived. If you can live it well while writing and publishing, while dancing and teaching dance, while painting and exhibiting — if you can live it well while making use of your brain, your heart, and your muscles — that is excellent project management and a great deal!

I've loved working with my clients, and I continue to love my work. I hope that what I've learned will help you. But in order for it to help you, you will have to do some real work. Roll up your sleeves in the service of your best life in the arts!

Chapter 1

THE MIND KEY

Your first task as a creative person is to "mind your mind" and think thoughts that serve you. Doesn't it make sense to speak to yourself in ways that help you create more deeply and more regularly, that allow you to detach more effectively from the everyday chaos of ordinary life, that decrease your anxiety and negativity, and that remind you that you are in charge of showing up and making an effort?

Many of us do a poor job of minding our minds, of choosing to think in ways that serve us. We present ourselves with self-sabotaging thoughts and refuse to dispute those thoughts once they arise. If we all did a better job of noticing what we are thinking and making an effort to replace defensive and unproductive thoughts with more optimistic and more productive ones, we would live in less pain and give ourselves a much better chance of our dream life.

It is this simple: Notice what you are thinking, dispute

those thoughts that bad-mouth you or that send you careening in the wrong direction, and replace them with thoughts that better serve you. This is tremendously important!

You can use many useful strategies, available from the cognitive-behavioral school of therapy, to get a better grip on your mind and help yourself think more productively and positively. Here's one I've created.

Often you have a productive thought, but then you immediately follow it with an unproductive one that stops you in your tracks. This sounds like "I'd love to practice the piano" followed by "but I'm much too old to learn complicated piano music." Or "I want to get my novel written" followed by "but I don't really know what my novel is about." Or "I love my photographic collages" followed by "but lots of people are doing them."

People engage in this self-sabotage all the time, deciding that something matters to them and then talking themselves out of taking action. It is almost what we do best as a species. I would like you to notice how this dynamic works in your life. Look at your own defensiveness, self-unfriendliness, and self-sabotage when it comes to those things that matter most to you. Look at this pattern, and then change it.

Complete the following, filling in the x and y with your own responses: "I say that x matters to me. But I often follow that thought up with y thought, a thought that does not serve me. I no longer want to countenance that thought." You may have more than one self-unfriendly y thought — you may have lots of them! By all means include as many y thoughts as you like in your response. The clearer you are on the things you say to yourself that don't serve you, the better will be your chances of extinguishing them.

Here is how some of my creativity coaching clients completed this exercise:

"I say that making art and selling my artwork matter to me. But I often follow that thought up with the thought that my artwork is not good enough to be considered attractive to buyers, a thought that does not serve me. I no longer want to entertain that thought. I will be open to opportunities to create and market my art, and I will make an effort to gain the support of art patrons."

"I say that being organized matters to me. But I often follow that thought up with the thought that I will take time to organize my work space some time in the future, a thought that does not serve me. I no longer want to entertain that thought. I am taking the time to organize every day so that my studio feels peaceful and spacious, with a good energy flow."

"I say that writing my screenplay and revising my novel and sending out articles are important to me. But I often follow up that thought with 'What does any of it really matter?' In the past few years, I've come up against so many roadblocks. It doesn't feel like I matter to anyone. My husband is sick and needs my attention. Maybe concentrating on more basic needs is the most important thing to do — cleaning, gardening, exercising. But I realize that the only sure way I can fail at my writing is if I stop. The thought of quitting doesn't serve me because it prevents any success from ever happening. I no longer want to entertain the thought of stopping."

"I say that making and marketing my art matters to me. But I often follow that up with thoughts that I don't have anything important to say, that I can't decide which ideas to work on, that I'm too unoriginal, and that if I were to succeed I would have to be too social. These thoughts don't serve me. I no longer want to countenance them."

"I say that fiber craft matters to me, but I often follow that thought up with the following ones: that I'm too tired to knit; that it's too troublesome to gather the materials; that I don't know what I'm doing; that I'm not making art, I'm just following instructions; that I don't have the right tools; that I'm a poser and a pretender; and that I'll do it wrong. These thoughts do not serve me and I no longer want to countenance them."

"I say that music matters to me. But I often follow that up with the thought that I can't afford to dedicate myself to it, that there are more important things in life, that I'm not good enough anyway, and that there are a lot of other things I'm interested in and almost anything pays better than music, which generally pays close to nothing. I no longer want to countenance those thoughts."

I'm sure you can see how this process of telling off the thoughts that do not serve you will help you to create more often and more deeply and will improve your relationship to the art marketplace. Complete this x-y exercise, and then put the results into practice.

Creating depends on having a mind quiet enough to allow ideas to bubble up. Living a successful, healthy life as an artist requires that your self-talk align with your goals and your aspirations. Your job is to quiet your mind and extinguish negative self-talk. These are your two most important tasks if you want a shot at your best life in the arts. Here are some handy tips:

1. *Recognize that you are the only one who can get a grip on your mind.* There is no pill to take. There is no one to consult. There is nothing to read. You must mind your mind. You can let your thoughts do whatever they want and go off in any direction, or you can say, "No, that thought doesn't serve me." Only you can do that work.

2. *Recognize that you do not have to accept, tolerate, or countenance a thought just because you thought it.* You may have the thought, "Wow, John really made me angry at work today!" Then it is your choice whether to brood about John or whether to get on with your novel. It may be easier to brood about John than to

write your novel, so you may have powerful reasons to stay angry. It's your choice.

When we say something to ourselves like "My novel stinks" or "I won't play well tonight," we believe that thought just because we thought it. But many of our thoughts are simply not true, and even if they are true, they may not serve us.

3. *Listen to what you say to yourself.* If you can't hear your own thoughts, you can't get rid of the ones that aren't serving you. If you can't admit to yourself that you are constantly thinking that life is a cheat, that you've badly disappointed yourself by wasting so much time, or that you hate to be criticized, you won't be able to dispute and extinguish those thoughts. Yes, it can be extremely painful to admit to them, but it is better to grapple with them than to let them cycle endlessly.

4. *Decide if what you are telling yourself serves you.* You are not looking at the truth or falsity of a thought but rather at whether the thought is or isn't serving you. Countless true thoughts do not serve us. All the following may be true thoughts that nevertheless do not serve you to think: "I might have written ten books by now"; "Writing a novel is hard"; "Selling a novel is hard"; "I'm not sure I have it in me either to write a novel or to sell a novel." None of those thoughts, even if true, serve you. The only thought that serves you, if you want to write a novel, is "I am off to my novel!"

5. *When you decide that a thought doesn't serve you, dispute it and dismiss it.* It can seem very strange at first to dispute your own thoughts. Yet dispute them you must. Get in the habit of saying to yourself, "That was an interesting thought. Does it serve me?" If you know or suspect that it doesn't, dismiss it out of hand. Do not linger over it! This sounds like "That thought

doesn't serve me and I am dismissing it!" Mean it when you say it!

6. *When a thought that doesn't serve you lingers, actively combat it.* Some thoughts just won't go away. Maybe it's "No one wanted my first novel, and my second novel is an even more difficult sell, so why in heaven's name am I writing it?" You may not be able to get rid of this thought simply by snapping your fingers. Then do more than snap your fingers — fight the thought tooth and nail. Maybe you'll have to write out the ten reasons why this book may be wanted. Maybe you'll have to chat seriously with yourself about self-publishing. You must battle brooding, clinging, disabling thoughts — or else you will be thinking them regularly.

7. *After you've disputed and dismissed a thought, think a thought that does serve you.* Creating thought substitutes is an important part of the process. These substitutes can be tailored to the situation, or they can be simple global affirmations that you create once and use over and over again, such as "I'm perfectly fine," "Back to work," "Right here, right now," or "Process." Because for so many of us the default way of thinking is negative, self-critical, and injurious, we want to create and use thought substitutes that help prevent our brain from conjuring up its usual distortions and distractions.

8. *Get in the smart habit of extinguishing unproductive self-talk even before it arises.* Often we know when a thought is coming. Maybe you've been waiting to hear from an editor who said she would call on Tuesday, and now it's Friday. You know that if she doesn't call today, you are certain to begin thinking thoughts like "She's never going to call," "She's about to reject my work," and "I can't stand all this waiting." You *know*

these thoughts are coming. So extinguish them now and replace them with "I'm spending the weekend working on my new pet project! And I won't think about that editor until Monday!" How many times have you *known* that a thought that doesn't serve you is coming and let yourself think it anyway? It's time to stop doing that.

9. *Engage in active cognitive support.* This means creating the thoughts that you want to be thinking and then thinking them. These thoughts might include all of the following: "I paint every single morning"; "I'm going to succeed"; "I know how to make meaning"; "I'm lavishing my love and attention on my current painting"; "I'm not afraid of process"; "I show up"; "I take the risks that I need to take, with my work and in the marketplace"; "I am creating a body of work"; "I am a painter." You can think thoughts like these if you choose to think them.

You may never have thought about the possibility of getting a grip on your mind. I hope that you'll seriously consider it now. Here are some features of your mind that you most likely have always believed weren't in your control. Want to wrest back control of them?

Are you easily distracted? Probably you think that the things that distract you simply *are* distractions. But *distraction* is just a word you yourself have invented for the something that has happened or is happening. Yes, a truck has rumbled by — but that is only a distraction if you feel inclined to be distracted. Otherwise, you just look up and then you return to your creative work. Because creating is hard and because we are often secretly looking for reasons to stop, we turn our cat's walking by into a distraction and stop to watch her. You can change your mind about doing that.

Do you lose focus a lot and mentally wander off? Most

often this occurs because we don't know what comes next in the work, and as a result we grow anxious. It is in your power to regain your focus by recognizing that you've gotten a little anxious and by employing some techniques to reduce your anxiety and to talk yourself back to work. Managing creative anxiety of this sort is one of your most important tasks, and I recommend that you begin to employ one or two anxiety-management techniques from the more than twenty I provide in *Mastering Creative Anxiety*. Manage your anxiety, and you will do a better job of getting a grip on your mind.

Do you often feel mentally fatigued? This is different from being physically fatigued. Sometimes we're mentally fatigued because we've been using our brain all day, and that's pretty analogous to getting physically tired. But more often we get mentally fatigued as a result of feeling taxed by the work directly in front of us. That is, the work in front of us daunts us, and this tires us. The simple solution is to take a microbreak. Rather than straining more and getting more mentally tired, leave the work — with the intention of returning.

Do you tell yourself things such as "I can't paint today because the plumber is coming"? This is just a thought, and as just a thought it can be disputed and dismissed. It is completely within your power to hear yourself say, "I can't paint today because the plumber is coming," laugh out loud, and dismiss that thought with a new thought — for instance, "How ridiculous! The plumber isn't coming *for four hours*! Off I go to paint!"

Do you leave your work too easily and too soon? Perhaps you've had a small, anxious feeling or a thought that doesn't serve you, such as "Gee, I don't know what comes next." Maybe you've gotten a little anxious because you have come to a spot in your novel where you don't know what happens next and you don't want to do the wrong thing. That's a place where writers typically find a reason to leave the work. Instead of finding such a reason, you can say to yourself, "I'm going to walk around the house ten times, and then come right back." That's the essence of getting a grip on your mind.

Maybe you think that true thoughts can't be dismissed — or even that they shouldn't be dismissed. Well, often they can and they should. Just because you've had a thought that is objectively true doesn't mean you have to give it any credence. You might have a thought like "Wow, it's hard to get a literary agent!," which is true enough — but if you give that thought credence you're likely to stop writing. If a thought like that flits through your mind, you must instantly dismiss it as not serving you, replace it with your substitute thought (which might be "Back to writing!" or "I'm perfectly fine!"), and get back to work.

Many other challenges that you've decided you can't fix, for example, general mental confusion or attention deficit disorder, are likely much more in your control than you imagine. You can become a much smarter, calmer thinker and a much better self-advocate if you switch your head right now and decide to get a grip on your mind.

Feelings and Thoughts

Sometimes we can think a useful thought only after a painful feeling has subsided. The feeling may be too powerful for us to think clearly in the split second of feeling it. That is the way nature built us, to have powerful feelings that can trump thought. However, when that feeling *has* subsided, then it is our job to decide what we want to think. Here are two examples of what I mean.

Mary sent her slides off to a gallery where she had high hopes for representation. What she got back was a terse email: "Your work isn't up to our standards."

Mary stopped painting for the next three years.

Such dramatically unfortunate events happen all too often in the lives of artists. One sharp criticism can derail an artist not only for far too long but sometimes altogether, making him completely doubt that he has the right or the wherewithal to be a professional artist — or any kind of artist at all. The consequences of receiving this kind of blow are so severe primarily because of our powerful initial reaction to them, one that is often out of scale with the incident.

When someone says, either in veiled language or in no uncertain terms, that you are an idiot, that you have no talent, that you're mediocre, that you're a hack, that you're derivative, that you're... fill in the blank... you *will* have a reaction. Often it is a whole-body, hard-to-tolerate emotional reaction that shifts your world.

Virtually everyone has a strong, visceral reaction to being criticized, humiliated, or shamed. These powerful, automatic whole-body reactions, like our blushing response or our fight-or-flight response, are fundamental, hardwired parts of who we are. Maybe some very advanced human being can avoid feeling these things; maybe some very detached human being can avoid feeling these things. But the rest of us feel them. It will feel as if something tremendously large and bad has happened — and yet all that has *really* happened is that we are having a feeling.

Once we have that feeling, the ball is in our court. What are we going to do *next*? What you do next may affect how you spend the next year or even the rest of your life. If you take this pain in without doing anything to defuse it, you may lose a great deal of time or, if you manage to continue creating, work much less strongly than you otherwise might. Much better is the following. When a whole-body explosion of bad feeling erupts in you, use the following three-step technique to calm yourself down and to get a grip on the situation.

First, acknowledge that something happened. We are amazingly adept at being defensive creatures who can deny almost anything. We can make believe that we didn't drink that whole bottle of Scotch in one sitting; we can make believe that we hold no animosity toward our rageful, hurtful parents; we can make believe that getting to the studio once a month is really enough. Do not deny that something just happened. Acknowledge that you got slapped in the face, that it felt more like a blow to the gut, and recognize that you suddenly found yourself awash in stress chemicals, negative thoughts, and bad feelings. *Admit that something happened.*

Second, *doubt that anything really important happened.* You will be able to do this only after the initial pain has subsided. For the first few seconds or minutes of being blindsided, we can't help but stand in pain. But then slowly we are able to acknowledge that we received a bad blow. This acknowledgment allows a fierce determination not to let one person's opinion matter so much. Decide that your basic armament is a thick skin and that your basic orientation is "*I* decide these matters!" This may be hard to say — or believe — in the first five minutes after the blow, but after that it is your job to remind yourself that self-determination is your orientation of choice.

Third, engage in a courageous personal assessment of the situation. You may well not be able to engage in this assessment until later that evening, the next day, or the weekend, which is just fine. It is hard to engage in a truthful personal assessment until we have simmered down a bit. But once we've calmed down, we can do exactly that.

Let's say a visitor comes into your studio and says, "Wow, these paintings are pretty dead!" Two days later, if you are willing to look the matter in the eye, you may be able to come to your own true assessment of the situation. That assessment might be, "Ridiculous!" Or, "Yes, I see how trying to copy my really alive photographic collages onto the canvas has produced some fairly dead paintings. I've known that for a while. Okay, now I fully accept that truth. I can't do that any longer. I see that the photographic collages are my real work and don't need to be recopied!" *You* decide what you believe is true or

11

false about the accusation made, making sure not to err on the side of unnecessarily doubting yourself just because someone launched an attack.

Not a single one of these steps is easy. Acknowledging the blow is not easy. Refusing to care is not easy. Truthfully assessing is not easy. But harder still is losing the next year or your whole painting life. These blows come regularly. Know how you are going to deal with them so that they don't blindside you and ruin your year (or life).

Let's consider a second example. Here the feelings are less intense and their meaning less clear, but ultimately they prove just as disconcerting. Say that you have a studio mate with whom you get along pretty well. Her paintings look nothing like yours, so you aren't competing; she isn't chatty; she has no habits that annoy you. But one day she comes over to your side of the studio, watches you work for a while, and then says with a critical air, "You know, your sky would work better if you varied the tones more."

This is no huge insult; it may not be an insult at all. Even though she said it with a critical air, she may have been trying to be helpful. Be that as it may — and while you understand that the event was no big deal — you discover that you are starting to arrive at the studio at times when you think she won't be there.

The question of whether or not she will be there is beginning to prey on you. You find yourself dreaming up things to say to clear the air or to give her a piece of your mind. Then one day you realize that you're trying to avoid her at all costs. Shortly thereafter you stop going to the studio at all.

Maybe you can't quite say what's affecting you so much. You know intellectually that not much happened and that you shouldn't allow such a small event to keep you from your own studio. Yet that's exactly what's happened. You feel sheepish and childish and angry and...stuck.

You try to fathom what happened and what bothers you

so. Is it that now you feel watched? Is it the worry that she will speak that way again? Is it some sense of betrayal regarding the etiquette of studio sharing (although *betrayal* seems like a very over-the-top word for such a small event)? Is it no longer being able to experience your studio as a private place?

Whatever the reasons, you are stuck. Keeping the studio but not going to it can't be the best answer. What can you do? Your choices are the following: paint there anyway, or move. Maybe you could create a partition. Maybe there are some other practical answers. But probably the real choices are to paint there or move.

You probably don't need to have a conversation with your studio mate to clear the air — it is your reaction that is the problem, not her behavior, which was hardly egregious. So the work is either the heavy lifting of moving your studio or the heavy lifting of getting a grip on your mind. The latter is the more valuable labor.

Try to notice the exact thoughts that make it so hard to come to the studio. Maybe one is "I just can't be there anymore." Actually hearing that you are saying this to yourself is important. Once you hear that thought clearly, you're likely to want to respond, "Really?" or "How ridiculous!" Then you can create a thought substitute, which in this case might sound like "Of course I can still be there!" This careful cognitive work, in which you hear a thought that isn't serving you, dispute it, and substitute the thought you actually want to be thinking, is the essence of getting a grip on your mind.

Having a studio mate or mates is a special variation of working in public. Life is not quite the same with someone else in the room. Just as you must learn how to deal with gawkers if you paint en plein air, you must learn how to be "private in public" in a shared-studio situation. If the issues with your studio mates are large and intractable, that's one thing. But if they are relatively minor, then it's your job to talk yourself down from turning small irritations and modest skirmishes into dramas that cost you your ability to paint in your own studio.

Maybe you'll still get a knot in your stomach as you enter the studio. Maybe catching sight of your studio mate when you'd hoped she'd be elsewhere will bring you down a bit. These feelings are the cost of doing business and the cost of being human. Decide that you will weather them, not over-dramatize the situation, and paint in your lovely studio.

It is too much unnecessary work to run from studio to studio if something relatively minor is making you flee. Stay put instead. You don't want to lose the next six months changing studios when you could be painting instead.

Thinking over Time

I've focused so far on the matter of dealing with thoughts that don't serve you and following up powerful disruptive feelings with right thinking. Let me touch on another important aspect of getting a grip on your mind: getting in the habit of pursuing the creative ideas that interest you and matter to you.

Most would-be creative folks do not allow themselves to productively obsess about one idea and instead keep switching from idea to idea, enthusiasm to enthusiasm, and project to project. They do this in large measure because, usually unwittingly, they are afraid to really bite into one thing and stay there for as long as it takes to elaborate the idea and finish the project. (I've chatted about this at length in my book *Brainstorm: Harnessing the Power of Productive Obsessions*, so I don't want to repeat myself here.)

We *need* to obsess about the creative work that matters to us, and if we refuse to orient ourselves in the direction of our big ideas and our hardest work, we will end up living with small ideas and less fulfilling work. The following vignette from my creativity coaching practice illustrates what I mean.

How the Brain Doesn't Work

Robert was a neuroscientist. He taught at a prestigious state college, published articles in the area of stress and the brain, and had a good reputation. But he felt that something important was missing from his life — worthy intellectual work. He blamed his problem on his funding requirements.

"The way my world works," he began, "you look around and see what might be funded. You check out the landscape. In any given moment some things are hot and other things are cold. Maybe minority health issues are hot, and so you try to figure out if the work you want to do on stress and the brain can somehow be married to minority health issues. Or maybe it's a mind-body moment in the funding world — you say to yourself, 'Hm, how can I make that work? Maybe do a study that includes some meditation.' That's the way it works."

"Funding is that important?"

"Funding is that important. Funding is the whole game. It's God. It's everything."

"But you have a tenured position. Aren't you set?"

"Yes and no. I have a nice salary and a secure position. But this is a research institution. At a certain kind of small liberal arts college I could just teach. Here I have to run a lab and keep it running. I have graduate students to support. I have a whole business to run within my department. Teaching is so completely secondary that I sometimes forget that I do it."

I nodded. "And the issue is?"

"That I don't get any real thinking done." He shifted in his chair. "It's all thinking done to serve an end. I end up writing article after article based on study after study, rather than writing a book based on some serious reflection. It isn't so much that I'm sure I have anything to contribute. It's more that I want to experience riding the white water of a long, thoughtful argument about something. It doesn't have to be *The Origin of Species*. But I would like to say something."

"You may have the process backward."

"Meaning?"

"You probably need the 'something' to obsess about. That you aren't sure that you have anything to contribute is a telling admission. I'm guessing you have a hunch that if you could get permission from yourself to just think, rather than always serving your funding needs, that something would come to you. But maybe it's the other way around. Maybe you need to conjure up that something, something worth obsessing about, and the obsessing would begin."

He thought about that.

"What do you really want to bite into?" I continued. "Or, to use your metaphor, what white water do you want to ride?"

He continued thinking. "That may be the problem," he said quietly. "I've been framing the problem as chasing too many grants. But maybe the problem is that I don't have any something."

"That could be."

I let him wrestle with the specter that he had nothing to say and nothing to contribute.

"Neuroscience," he said after a while, "is something you can fiddle with and manipulate to suit your purposes. You can say that some connection exists between x and y and spend a decade playing with your suppositions, even if there is no chance for them to be proved accurate. Because my world has this *Alice in Wonderland* quality to it, it's hard to take any idea seriously — even my own. The average person has no idea how much we just make things up. I don't want to just make up another thing."

I nodded. "That's entirely admirable. But it's also a paralyzing vision. The question becomes, despite the unreality, fancifulness, and fraudulence around you, 'Is there something worth saying?' Is there?"

"There is. I could write a book about the misuse of research studies. Though there aren't seven people in the world who would want to read it."

"That's very noble," I agreed. "But let's table that for a second and see if there's some intellectual work that's worthy and interesting that doesn't take you down that path."

He thought about that. "I think I've been seeing my alternatives as more and more articles or this book. I don't know that I've been open to a big idea."

"Stay open now."

"Well, the trap in my field is always the following: to do a 'how the brain works' book that claims to tie everything together. The superintegrative unified field theory of neuroscience. There's always that lure!"

"Which would send you down the rabbit hole."

"Exactly. It would just be manipulating language so as to make believe that I had an answer."

"Okay. No 'how the brain works' book."

He grew downcast. "But I think that's actually the only worthy book to write, even though it can't and shouldn't be written. That makes me sad — that it's the book to write, though none of us know enough to write it."

"Maybe *that* is the book to write. The book about why a 'how the brain works' book can't be written. But..." I paused to get his attention. "But not written in an 'all those books on how the brain works are stupid' way but rather in a forward-looking way in which you point out what still needs to be known and how we can know it. That might feel worthy, affirmative, and intellectually challenging."

He stared at me. After a moment he smiled. "Well, that is one brilliant idea. I could obsess about that."

"You are already." I laughed. "The rest will fall into place... if you don't talk yourself out of it."

"I don't think I will," he said. "I think that is exactly the right idea and can't not be obsessed about it. If I am not thinking about this day and night I will be very surprised."

"But do show up to class," I said.

He laughed. "I have an inner clock that gets me to class," he said. "I don't have to spend many neurons on that. I get to spend them on this new thing — every single neuron I can gather!"

Screenplays Still to Come

Here's a second vignette to help illustrate what getting a grip on your mind looks like.

Sophie kept herself busy. She had children; she and her family moved to a new, larger house; she started a home consulting business. It all made sense — except for the disaster that she tried not to think about. She had come this close to succeeding as a screenwriter and could still succeed, given her connections, talent, and understanding of the business. But the marketplace had battered her so badly that she had given up on her dream.

She kept herself busy and most of the time managed not to think about her twin disappointments: her disappointment at the screenwriting marketplace for cavalierly mauling her scripts, and her disappointment at herself for letting that business reality stop her from persevering. The marketplace had failed her, and she had failed herself. All this pain and bile she tried to keep out of conscious awareness — where naturally it continued to eat at her.

In fact, she'd had some real successes. Three of her scripts had been turned into movies of the week, and the last of those three was about to air in a month or two. Sophie might have experienced these as real accomplishments, if only she hadn't hated what had become of each script. The finished movies were dreadfully dull and sappy. Each script had been doctored by a team of rewrite specialists, whose job it was to cut out the script's heart and replace it with the usual hack effects. The experience made her crazy.

Sophie came to see me about her consulting business and not her screenwriting life. She remarked only in passing that she'd previously sold three scripts but no longer pursued a screenwriting career. I knew we had to stop right there. When someone has invested that much meaning, done that much work, and had so many real successes in an art discipline, it's imperative to check in and see what's going on.

"I need to talk about the screenwriting for a minute," I said.

"Okay."

"Selling three scripts is a real accomplishment."

She grudgingly agreed.

"What happened?"

"They got butchered. The finished movies embarrassed me. I can't go through that hell again."

I nodded. "But you have other scripts ready to show?"

She heaved an enormous sigh. "I have three script ideas I love. I've worked a bit on all three of them, but I just don't want to subject them — subject me — to the butchery that happens when a studio gets its hands on a script. I can't stand picturing my beautiful work murdered by some rewrite team."

"Interesting," I said. "Interesting that you've chosen to go for words like *butchered* and *murdered*." I let that sink in for a moment. "I think your language is harming you," I said. "You've turned a real-world problem into an even worse cognitive problem. It's one thing to think about a script as your *baby*. It's another thing to start using the language of infanticide."

She thought about that. "It's what I feel."

"Language needs to serve you, not make problems harder. Don't you think?"

"Yes."

"You keep telling yourself that you hate the business, you hate the business, you hate the business. How often do you remind yourself that some beautiful movies get made?"

"Almost never. Never."

"Have you seen a beautiful movie this year?"

"Several — some from the big studios, lots by independent filmmakers, and a bushel of foreign ones. Some stunning movies."

"And when you see one of those, do you say, 'Oh, look, good movies get made'?"

"Never."

"You're cognitively hooked on hating the business. Is that serving you?"

Tears came. At first they were tears of sadness at having lost so much time through adopting a language of hatred. Then they became tears of relief. She understood that she could think about the film industry differently — and the difference was huge. She could think of it not only as a place where films got butchered but also as a place where beautiful films got made. That mental adjustment changed everything.

"All right," I said. "What do you want to do?"

It took her a bit of time to gather herself. Once gathered, however, she knew with perfect certainty what she wanted.

"One of my three script ideas I love to bits. I want to do the treatment for it and then start writing it. When it's ready I have people I want to show it to — I'm incredibly lucky in that regard."

"Talk me through your new language," I said.

She had to think about this. "I'm not going to use any *hate* or *kill* or *murder* language anymore. Instead…" She shook her head. "I'm not sure what I'm going to say when I think about those first three scripts. I don't know."

"Of course. No reason why good substitute language should come to you in a split second! But let's stay here. What might you say instead?"

"That…I had a learning experience."

"Okay."

"And that I sold three scripts! I can't seem to celebrate that. I just get fixated on..."

We both smiled.

"On how the studios murdered them," I said.

"On how the studios murdered them." She laughed.

I knew that she would return to the fray. Was she likely to get battered again? You bet! Might she yet see a future script turned into a beautiful movie? If she could watch her language, aligning it with her hopes and her ambitions and not with her disgust for the industry, it was entirely possible. Those three sold scripts certainly meant something — even if the movies that got made left everything to be desired.

Your Brain Your Way

I am painfully aware of how often creative and performing artists think thoughts that do not serve them and how often they fail to understand that it is their job to get a grip on their minds.

Most creative and performing artists stop themselves every day with uncontrolled self-talk that does not serve them. A single thought like "It's too late" or "My work doesn't really matter" can cost you a year or a decade. If you do not continually monitor the quality and kindness of your thoughts, you can't possibly lead your best life in the arts.

Try actively thinking a thought that you would like to think, for example, "I want to have many books published." Were you able to think that thought? Try thinking a thought that doesn't serve you, for example, "I can't get published because there is so much competition." Then try disputing that thought. Were you able to think that thought and *then dispute it*?

Try thinking a thought that doesn't serve you, for example, "I can't get published because there is so much competition." Now create a thought that serves you better, one that might substitute for that first thought — for example, "There's a lot of competition, but I don't fear competition!" Were you able to create both the negative thought and the thought substitute?

Identify some fairly regular thoughts that don't serve you. Next, create a more useful thought to substitute for each of the unproductive thoughts you just identified. Can you see yourself identifying unproductive thoughts, disputing them, and replacing them with more useful thoughts? If you can't, why can't you?

Discuss getting a better grip on your mind with yourself. What's your game plan? Because you will need one. Every creative person, being a human being, is plagued by thoughts that do not serve him or her. You can bet on it. What are you going to do?

Chapter 2

THE CONFIDENCE KEY

Both the creative act and the creative life require confidence. And life can rob you of confidence.

Let's say a teacher constantly humiliates you in front of the entire third-grade class. How much confidence is stolen from you during that excruciating year? How many other robberies occur during our childhood and our adulthood? Over time, how much confidence remains? If you've been robbed of confidence, you may experience an inability to conceive of and follow through on creative projects, a tendency to procrastinate, a fear of messes and of the unknown, and other assorted creativity killers.

Consider the following. A painter opens his email and is thrilled to find a note from someone who owns a nice gallery in a faraway city. The note explains that the gallery owner has visited the painter's website and loves the painter's work but can't find the painter's prices posted. What, the gallery owner wonders, are the artist's prices?

This question sends the artist into a tizzy, since he has no idea if his prices are perhaps ridiculously high or, quite possibly, ridiculously low (which is why he has avoided posting them on his site). He stews about the matter for several days, feeling his usual lack of confidence grow exponentially. Finally he visits his best friend, a successful artist with a great deal of confidence. "What should I do?" the painter cries. "I know I'm blowing this opportunity by not replying, but I don't know what to say!"

His friend shakes his head and laughs. "Get me the gallery's phone number," he says. The painter does that. His friend picks up the phone, dials, and says, "I represent Jack Sprat. You emailed him about his prices. We are setting new prices this year and would love your input. His recent works, the ones you saw on his site, are each two feet by three feet. How would you consider pricing them?" The painter watches as his friend listens, occasionally nods, and finally says, "Thanks! We'll follow up on that in a day or two."

When his friend hangs up, the painter almost leaps on him. "What did he say?" he cries. "That he would be inclined to charge $4,800 retail," his friend replies, "and that he would like to try out two of your paintings, the blue one and the red one." The painter is beside himself with joy. Then, suddenly, he exclaims, "How did you *do* that? You just picked up the phone and called!" At this, his friend shakes his head. "Jack," he says, "how could you *not* do that? These things are incredibly simple...unless anxiety turns them into monsters!"

Confidence throughout the Creative Process

Not sure what confidence actually looks like as it applies to the creative act and the creative process? Here is a thumbnail sketch of the ten stages involved:

1. *Wishing.* I'm conceptualizing wishing as a kind of precontemplation stage in which you haven't really decided that you mean to create and haven't bought into the rigors of the creative process and are still wishing that creating could somehow be easier. You dabble at making art, you don't find your efforts very satisfying, you don't feel that you go deep all that often, and so on.

   The confidence that you need to manifest during this stage of the process is the confidence *that you are equal to the rigors of creating.* If you don't confidently accept the reality of process, the reality of difficulty, and the reality of effort, and if you can't say with confidence, "Yes, I agree to all that!," you may never really get started.

2. *Incubation/contemplation.* During this second stage of the process, you need to remain open to what wants to come rather than defensively settling on a first idea or on an easy idea. The task is remaining open and not settling for something that relieves your anxiety and your discomfort. The confidence needed here is the confidence to *stay open.*

3. *Choosing your next subject.* You can call this a stage or a moment, but however you conceptualize it, choosing is a crucial part of the creative process. In this stage you have to decide what you are working on, and then work on it with energy and intention. At some point you need the confidence to say, "I am ready to work *on this.*" You need the confidence to name a project clearly (even if that naming is "Now I go to the blank canvas without a preconceived idea and just start"), to commit to it, and to make sure that you aren't *leaking confidence* even as you choose this project.

4. *Starting your work.* When you launch a new creative work, you start with certain ideas, certain hopes and

enthusiasms, and certain doubts and fears — that is, you start with an array of thoughts and feelings, some positive and some negative. The confidence you need at that moment is the confidence *that you can weather all those thoughts and feelings* and the confidence *to go into the unknown.*

5. *Working.* Once you are actually working on your creative project, you enter into the long process of fits and starts, ups and downs, excellent moments and terrible moments — the gamut of human experiences that attach to real work. For this stage you need the confidence *that you can deal with your doubts and resistances* and the confidence *that you can handle whatever the work throws at you.*

6. *Completing.* At some point you will be close to completing the work. It is often hard to complete what we start because then we are obliged to appraise it, deal with the rigors of showing and selling, enter into the void of being without a new project, and so on. The confidence required during this stage is the confidence to *weather the very ideas* of appraisal, criticism, rejection, disappointment, and everything else that we fear will be coming our way once we announce that the work is done, and the confidence to actually *be finished.*

7. *Showing.* If we are creating work that we intend to send out into the world, then the time comes when we must show it. The confidence needed here is not only the confidence to weather the *ideas* of appraisal, criticism, rejection, and disappointment but also the confidence to weather the *reality* of appraisal, criticism, rejection, and disappointment. Like so many other manifestations of confidence, the basic confidence here sounds like "Bring it on!" You are agreeing to let

the world do its thing and announcing that you can survive any blows the world delivers.

8. *Selling.* A confident seller can negotiate, think on her feet, make pitches and presentations, advocate for her work, and explain why her work is wanted. You don't have to be overconfident, exuberant, or over-the-top — you simply need to be a *calmly confident seller*, someone who first makes a thing and then sells it in a businesslike fashion.

9. *New incubation and contemplation.* While you are showing and selling your completed works, you are also incubating and contemplating new projects and starting the process all over again. The confidence required here is the confidence *that you have more good ideas in you.* Sometimes we feel as if the thing we just finished contained everything we had to say and that now we are creatively bereft, even doomed. You want to confidently assert that you have plenty more to say and do — even if you don't know what that something is quite yet.

10. *Simultaneous and shifting states and stages.* I've made the creative process sound neat and linear, but usually it is anything but. Often we are stalled on one thing, contemplating another thing, trying to sell a third thing, and so on. Much in our creative life goes on simultaneously and shifts from moment to moment. The confidence needed *throughout the process* is the quiet, confident belief that you can stay organized, successfully handle all the thoughts and feelings going on inside you, get your work done, and *manage everything.* This is a juggler's confidence — it is you announcing, "You bet that I can keep all these balls in the air!"

Manifest confidence *throughout the creative process.* Failing to manifest confidence in any stage will stall the process.

Confidence and Boundary Issues

Often a creative person's lack of confidence plays itself out as boundary issues, that is, as the way she gives herself away to other people or as the way she enters into volatile relationships with them.

As artists, we require solitude, probably more than the next person. But we also require human warmth, friendships, and marketplace advocacy. Life can grow too cold if we live it completely alone, and our career suffers if we avoid interactions with the people who might help us and who might appreciate our art. So, although we may consider ourselves introverts and feel happiest keeping ourselves company, we have many interpersonal needs — and we want to meet them from a place of confidence.

How should we relate to our fellow artists, to gallery owners, to potential collectors, to publishers, and to the other people whose cooperation, consideration, and sometimes friendship we seek? We achieve these things by doing a good job of balancing genuine warmth and intimacy with healthy self-protection. It will not benefit us to consider other people the enemy and to interact with them aggressively or defensively, but it will also not benefit us to naively and unquestioningly put our complete trust in our fellow human beings. People can love one another, and they can also harm one another. Virtually every shade of interaction, from the kindest to the cruelest, is part of the human repertoire. So we do have to be careful — but we also want to feel confident that our relationships *can work.*

One painter complained to me that her friends, the organizations where she volunteered her time, her family members, and the few gallery owners with whom she dealt regularly took advantage of her. I asked her what role she played in this unfortunate dynamic. She responded at length, but she never really answered the question. I wondered aloud if her very communication style — as evidenced by the way she had just responded to me — had developed over time to spare her from saying things directly and clearly. I wondered if she spoke evasively and at length to save herself from saying short, sweet, strong, confident things. She pondered this for a long moment and then agreed.

She admitted that she had a terrible time saying no to people or directly announcing what she wanted and needed. This inability, which she could easily trace to childhood dynamics, resulted in people walking all over her. In therapy, we might have explored the childhood part at great length; since this was coaching, I went directly to the solution. I asked her to try speaking in sentences of no more than six or seven words and to say in those sentences exactly what she meant.

Then we role-played. The first issue that came up was the way her husband, who had retired early, kept visiting her in her studio to chat about inconsequential matters. I asked her to craft a sentence of seven words or fewer that would communicate what she wanted to say to him: that her painting time was precious to her. Her first efforts were grotesquely long, apologetic, and weak. Finally, after many tries, she arrived at "I can't chat much while I'm working."

"Can you say that to him?" I asked.

"Yes," she replied.

"How does it feel?" I continued.

"Very, very scary."

Next we role-played a problem she was having with the fellow who did some printing work for her. He was the only person in her area equipped to do this work, and she liked both the work he did and his prices. But he was always inappropriate with her, saying things like "Most husbands don't understand their artist wives."

"What do you want to say to him?" I asked.

Having just practiced, she was now quicker to respond. "I need you to stop that," she said. "I am coming here to have prints made, period." She laughed. "That's two sentences, and one's a little long. But that's the idea, right?"

"That's exactly the idea," I agreed.

When we say that a person has boundary issues, we mean that he is doing one or the other of two inappropriate things: that he is insufficiently protecting his own being or that he is aggressively intruding on others. A constant apologist has one kind of boundary issue; a stalker has another. As an artist, you want to be mindful of how you relate to others and opt for the kind of strength that allows you to advocate for yourself and that protects you from the assaults of others.

This is your work; no one else can do it for you. By the stances you take, by the words you use, by the vibe you give off, you let people know that you will not be anybody's dishrag. You manifest your confidence by doing a good job at maintaining appropriate boundaries with all those with whom you interact.

Presenting Your Artist Self with Confidence

You may feel quite confident in many areas of your life but find yourself much weaker than you would like when you get to the canvas or when you need to talk to a gallery owner. A reasonable amount of general confidence isn't enough for an artist who wants to succeed. You need more than general confidence — you need confidence *as an artist*.

What happens if you aren't really confident as an artist? You may start relying on your first ideas and not go deep; you may flee the encounter completely; you may think small rather than large; you may give up at the first hint of trouble (which will come sooner rather than later); you may avoid the marketplace. Simply by not feeling confident enough in your abilities as an artist and in your abilities as a salesperson, you may do yourself and your career a great deal of harm.

What should you be confident about? It doesn't have to

be that a given project will succeed: you don't really want to attach to outcomes. It doesn't have to be that somehow you can avoid missteps, mistakes, and messes: nobody can avoid any of that, and that isn't how the process works anyway. What you should be confident about is that you are a legitimate human being with the right to be and the power to create. If you can find a way to feel confident about your legitimacy and your powerfulness, you will work better and sell better.

You may not actually *feel* very confident as you paint or write, as you advocate for your work, or as you present your work to prospective buyers, but even if you aren't feeling confident, you should keep confidence in mind as an aspiration. Aim for confidence, just as you aim for excellence in the work itself. It is that aura of confidence that propels one person past another in the marketplace. When someone is confident in his approach, you listen; when he hems and haws and shifts his feet, you look for the exit. When you portray yourself as not really counting, you're likely to be dismissed out of hand.

Apologizing for your work, hiding from potential buyers, avoiding marketplace interactions, dismissing yourself as soon as you can (as if beating others to the punch): these are all bad habits that you will want to change. To change a habit means to work on it for months and even years, not for just a few minutes. It is unlikely that, for example, you can suddenly start taking the opportunities offered to you just by snapping your fingers, if previously you have been unable to take them. You need to be on a lifelong strengthening program, a self-coaching regimen in which each day you remind yourself that you intend to manifest your strength and your confidence.

Remember: It is one thing to be quiet; it is another to be meek. It is one thing to be modest; it is another to be self-disparaging. It is one thing to be principled; it is another to live by the principle that everybody else comes first. You want to step out of the shadows and risk standing up for your work and your future. Maybe you doubt your work: either stop doubting it or create work that you doubt less. Maybe you doubt yourself: stop doubting yourself and, over time, create a version of yourself that you have no reason to doubt.

Present yourself with strength. If doing this doesn't come naturally to you, practice. Practice in your mind, in the mirror, or with an art buddy. Practice saying, "I love my new work." Practice saying, "If your gallery has an opening for one new artist, it should be me, and here's why." Practice saying, "I know that you collect contemporary surrealists, and I'm pushing the surrealism envelope, so you must visit my studio!" Practice saying, "Let me describe the nine ways in which I will be an asset to your gallery." Practice saying, "I am doing excellent work, and you should really take a look."

It is not just what you say — it is how you look at the world, how you think, and what you do. Either you are looking for opportunities to show your artwork or you aren't. Either you are mulling over new marketing ideas or you aren't. Either you are thinking about your next sales opportunities or you aren't. Either you are calculating what might work in the marketplace or you aren't. You are either a player in the game or a spectator in the stands. Either you are taking real action or you are fantasizing about what lucky break might come your way.

All this translates into a way of presenting yourself that is professional, savvy, energetic, proactive, eager, and decisive. Your intentions are clear: you intend to succeed. Your handshake is firm. You have people to interest and customers to acquire. Your first thoughts aren't "What should I say?" and "Where's the exit?" You know what to say, and you know where you mean to be: right here, right now, representing yourself in the brightest light possible.

Even if you don't actually *feel* confident, try to *act* confident. You may find yourself growing into that role and that persona!

Ten Confidence Boosters

Perhaps you want to begin some new creative projects or attempt some new ways of promoting yourself, but something is holding you back. Here are ten tips for expanding your repertoire of creative projects and/or your self-promotional efforts. If you do these things, your confidence will grow.

1. *Know what you currently do.* Because our lives rush along, providing us with little chance to catch up with ourselves, often we don't really know what we've been attempting or accomplishing. When was the last time you had a conversation with yourself about what sort of art you're making or what sort of marketing efforts you're attempting? It's harder to know what new things to try if you don't know what *current* things you're doing. Settle in and spend some real time discerning your current situation.

2. *Detach from the idea that there is one way to do things.* In part because it reduces our anxiety, we often decide to do things one way — paint one sort of painting, market in one particular way — and refuse to think about the desirability of other art or other marketing efforts that we might make. Maybe you think that only the gallery scene is for you and that marketing your art online is beneath your dignity. Try to let go of the idea that there is just one way to do things. Find the courage to investigate other ways of making art and marketing art, even those that at first glance look completely uncongenial. You might discover that one of these ways ignites some passion in you and instantly increases your confidence.

3. *Investigate your dislikes.* If you dislike realistic painting, *why* do you dislike it? If you dislike abstract painting, *why* do you dislike it? If you dislike talking to

gallery owners, *why* do you dislike this type of inter-action? If you dislike studio visits, *why* do you dislike them? We often make snap judgments about our likes and dislikes and subsequently never investigate them, responding instead with a knee-jerk reaction. Take a good, hard look at the things you claim to dislike and see if they really are so unlikeable. Turning some of those dislikes into likes may prove the exact equivalent of rekindling your desire and increasing your confidence.

4. *Investigate your fears.* We often hide from ourselves the fact that something is scaring us or making us anxious. Maybe we have real fears that our drawing skills aren't up to snuff. So we keep dodging that painful information and paint abstractly, not because we *genuinely* want to paint abstractly but because we know that our realistic paintings wouldn't measure up. It is very brave work, and very valuable work, to look your fears and anxieties in the eye. Only then will you understand your true situation. That understanding is bound to open the door to courageous new efforts — and new confidence.

5. *Articulate your possibilities.* What new art do you want to attempt? What new marketing efforts do you want to try? If you don't name them, it's unlikely you'll be able to pursue them. If, on the other hand, you can say clearly to yourself that you want to try your hand at some Calderesque mobiles or that you want to learn how to affiliate market your paintings, that clarity of expression will help you move in new directions — and make you both more enthusiastic and more confident.

6. *Make a strong choice.* Let's say that you want to make several kinds of art: some sculptures, a multimedia project, some monoprintings, and a new style that

involves personal history. It is exciting to want to do many things, but it can also prove paralyzing to have too many simultaneous choices. Choose *something* strongly without second-guessing whether it is the best choice and without grieving that you can't do *x* or *y* because you are doing *z*. Until we make strong choices of this sort, we tend not to get *anything* done. It may be exciting to imagine doing a lot of things, but it is actually more exciting to really *do* one thing — and making that strong choice is a confidence booster.

7. *Stretch in a new direction.* If you're moving in a genuinely new direction, that movement is likely to *feel* risky as well as exciting. Risky things actually feel risky in the body. Don't be surprised if your stomach gets queasy or your palms sweat — and don't use those feelings as an excuse to stop what you're attempting. Instead say, "Okay, I'm making myself anxious here — and that's okay. Onward!" If you've been painting your whole life and now you're starting to sculpt, isn't it likely that will feel like a stretch? Accept that reality!

8. *Accept being a beginner.* If you are trying something genuinely new to you — for example, you are moving from watercolors to acrylics or moving from studio visits to gallery efforts — you must accept that you are a beginner and that you will stammer more than you would like, stub your toe more than you would like, and on some days feel completely lost at sea. Do not let these realities become the excuses you use to return to more familiar ways. Expect them, accept them, and persevere! And maybe inject some beginner's passion into the process! Paradoxically enough, accepting that you are a beginner when you *are* a beginner will increase your confidence.

9. *Accept the reality of learning curves.* Not only are you a genuine beginner at this new painting style or

marketing technique, but you will also have to endure the learning curve that comes with any new effort. Just picture the learning curve required to go from your first piano lessons to playing Bach at Lincoln Center. Don't let the fact that a learning curve is coming daunt you or deter you. Accept the reality, forgive yourself on the days when you make "too little" progress, and keep the payoff in mind — your growth and success as an artist. You might even want to generate some enthusiasm and love for the very idea of a learning curve!

10. *Parlay what you already know.* Even though you may be a beginner at some new painting technique, composing style, or marketing strategy, you are not a beginner at life. You can parlay all that you've learned over the years and make your current experience that much easier. Remind yourself that you know a lot and that you intend to bring all that knowledge to your efforts, and you will do a much better job of maintaining your enthusiasm, optimism, focus, and confidence.

Confidence and Anxiety Management

It's often the case that even when we're reasonably confident on the inside, when it comes to accessing that confidence for some specific reason, like getting on with our painting or contacting a particular gallery, we can't seem to get there. Either we proceed very weakly, or we decide not to proceed at all.

What has typically happened is the following. We really did want to work on our painting or contact that gallery, and we knew that we should do that work because it served our meaning needs and matched our intentions. But as soon as we got ready, something welled up in us: that old culprit, anxiety.

Anxiety is the great stopper and the great silencer. We

get a little scared, a little doubtful, a little worried; we start to produce stress hormones in our body and all sorts of queasy, uncomfortable feelings; and suddenly our intention flies right out the window.

Most people are not very smart about anxiety, even though anxiety has repeatedly visited them. Instead of embracing that we are human, that we get anxious, and that we need to manage our anxiety or make our meaning despite our anxiety, we often act surprised that "something has happened" — namely, that our very inexact warning system against danger has leaped into operation. Why are we still *surprised* that we get anxious?

It is time to stop being surprised. It is time to become an anxiety master. If, being honest with yourself, you know that anxiety is a problem for you, that it robs you of confidence, and that it has gotten in the way of manifesting your intentions more times than you care to remember, now is the time to take responsibility for learning how to deal with that anxiety.

Unaddressed anxiety robs us of confidence. In order to regain the confidence that is "this close" to being available to you, you need to realize that anxiety is the culprit and announce to yourself either that you will manage it using the anxiety-management techniques I hope you will learn or that you will do what you need to do *while still feeling anxious*. We would not have wanted Eisenhower to stop planning D-day because he was feeling too anxious. Do not allow yourself to stop creating or to stop selling because you are feeling anxious.

Of course, better than just white-knuckling the situation is being able to reduce your anxiety or even, for that moment at least, eliminating it entirely. You want to manifest the courage necessary to get on with your art and your career even if you are feeling anxious; but even better is not to have to feel so anxious in the first place. This is possible!

In my book *Mastering Creative Anxiety* I describe more than twenty categories of anxiety-management strategies, everything from breathing techniques to cognitive techniques to relaxation techniques to discharge techniques. You can employ calming guided visualizations; you can use the technique called "disidentification" that's employed in a branch of therapy known as psychosynthesis; you can create useful ceremonies and rituals; you can learn how to reorient away from anxiety-producing stimuli. There are many, many techniques and strategies you can try!

But it isn't enough to read a book and nod your head in agreement as you recognize your situation. Rather, you want to choose one or two of the strategies offered and practice them and *own them* so that they are available to you when you grow anxious. You may want to run through the whole menu first and try out each one, at least a little bit, to see which one or two seem most congenial to you. Then commit to really learning and practicing the one or two you find most helpful.

Practice your new favorite anxiety-management strategy every day. Create situations in your mind's eye that you know are going to make you anxious, and, again in your mind's eye, see yourself using your anxiety-management strategy and effectively reducing your anxiety. This kind of visual rehearsal can prove very effective in helping you finally get a better grip on your anxiety — and increase your confidence.

Many productive, brilliant artists are anxious people. They nevertheless manage to manifest the confidence and courage they need to create and sell — sometimes by quelling their anxiety in harmful ways, such as drinking too much. If you work at really learning and owning a few useful anxiety-management strategies and becoming a personal-anxiety expert, you may discover that you have proved the exception: you've become an artist who can deal with anxiety in effective, nonharmful ways and who can manifest the confidence you need whether or not you are feeling anxious.

The Show She Might Have Had

All people come with a past and a personality. Marsha was no exception. Her sister's accidental death at the age of twelve, and her family's collapse after that terrible tragedy, robbed Marsha of something vital: joy, confidence, and hope for her future. It also seemed to rob her of her health. She suffered from a chronic earache, and it made painting, which was the light of her life, painful and difficult. So she produced little — lovely things, but only occasional things.

At one point several of these occasional things had accumulated. Marsha was then in her late twenties. She had a friend by the name of Meredith who had a friend by the name of Valerie. Valerie ran a small, prestigious gallery, and Meredith suggested that Valerie see Marsha's work. A studio visit was arranged. Valerie arrived. Marsha, her ear aching and her nerves raw, awkwardly showed Valerie around. It didn't take long, and soon Valerie left. Something about that visit and the ensuing silence provoked Marsha to come and see me.

"How did the visit go?" I asked after we were settled.

"It was pleasant. Fine."

"What did she say?"

"That she liked my work a lot."

"And?"

"And what?"

"Did you ask her if she wanted to give you a show?"

"No! She didn't seem that interested."

"She said that she liked your work a lot. But she didn't seem that interested?"

"Exactly. I sensed that she was just being polite. She didn't have much to say about my work as she was looking at it."

"What did she say? Besides that she liked it a lot?"

"Oh, she said this and that. She thought that I had a tremendous color sense, that I had a unique perspective, things like that."

"And that sounded like mere politeness?"

"Well, she didn't say that she loved anything! And she didn't…I don't know…have a lot to say."

I almost smiled. "What would you have said to Van Gogh about *Starry Night*?" I asked after a moment.

Marsha shrugged. "I don't know. That I loved it."

"And? What else?"

"I don't know. Maybe nothing."

"Not 'What an interesting way to paint stars'?"

"No. God, no!"

"Not 'How much you've crammed into a small canvas!'?"

"No!"

"And since you would have stood there mute or nearly mute, he should have taken that to mean that you were just being polite when you said you loved it?"

She frowned.

"Maybe she really liked my work," she said after a long moment.

"So you'll get in touch with her?"

Marsha closed right down.

"Well…"

"Yes?"

"My paintings are of very different sizes. They wouldn't make for a coherent show."

"So, you're mind-reading again?"

"Mind-reading? No. I just know how shows work."

"Is that right? There's a show at the Modern." I mentioned the name of a well-known artist. "You've seen it?"

"Yes."

"What are the sizes of the paintings in that show?"

Marsha thought about that. "Every size under the sun. Miniatures. Huge things."

"And so?"

"She's famous. She can get away with different sizes."

"I see. She started out famous?"

"No."

"And all her early works were of one size?"

"No. I'm sure they weren't."

"So you'll get in touch with Valerie?"

"I've taken too long to get back to her," she said. "I missed that train."

"And you know that how?"

"Just intuition. I'm extremely intuitive."

"How long has it been?"

"A month. Almost two."

"Do you want a show?"

That stopped her. After a bit she said, "Maybe I don't." It was a very breezy answer. "I'm not sure her gallery is really right for me. I should go check it out again. Plus, it's so expensive to frame things — she didn't say who would have to pay for the framing. I'm sure it would have to be me. I don't know if I want to pay for the framing and then not sell anything and get more depressed. So, no, probably not, probably I don't want a show at her gallery."

"I see. But the same issues would arise with any gallery. So you don't want a show at any gallery?"

She thought about that. Suddenly she brightened. "Yes, I think that's right! I think that I don't actually want a gallery show. I think that I want something different — a more human way to show my work. Maybe some sort of collective effort — maybe I should start a group gallery in an alternative space. But I don't have the strength for that. So I would have to find a group that already exists. But the ones that already exist are probably cliquish, and I don't do that well with groups…"

We continued in this vein until the end of the session. I plugged away at wondering aloud how it could be a bad thing to contact Valerie and secure a show at Valerie's good gallery. Marsha countered each suggestion with her reasons why such a show was either a bad idea or a complete impossibility. At the end of the session she smiled a small, wry smile, as if to say, "I'm really difficult, aren't I?" Or maybe her smile meant, "I think I won. How's that for a victory?"

Had we made any progress? Marsha was certainly not a changed person. Still, because we had been talking about the right things, I would have bet that a seed was planted. If we had been witness to her inner dialogue, I'm sure we would have overheard a conversation between her frightened, irritable, stubbornly negative everyday voice and that other voice, the one that guided the painting, appreciated life, and would have loved a little success.

I had high hopes for our next meeting.

Increasing Your Confidence

Describe in your own words what you are going to do to increase your confidence. Here are some suggestions to get you started:

- You might begin by identifying some situations in which you manifested your confidence and some situations in which your confidence failed you. What made the difference in each case?
- You might discuss with yourself the idea of acting confident even if you don't feel confident.
- You might create a personal list of efforts you are going to make to increase your confidence — your own game plan.

However you tackle this challenge, please tackle it. Virtually every creative person needs more confidence than he or she is manifesting. Your best life in the arts is dependent on your confidence level.

Chapter 3

THE PASSION KEY

M any creative people and most would-be creative people are interested in their artistic projects but not *passionately* interested in them. There is a huge difference here, and a big problem.

Mere interest does not sustain motivational energy, and it isn't a match for the obstacles that arise as you try to create. You need passionate interest in order to generate energy and to see you through the rigors of creating.

Passion and its synonyms — *love, curiosity, enthusiasm, excitement,* and *energy* — are vital to the creative process. Though it is possible to create without passion, your art will suffer, and the likelihood of your continuing over the long haul is greatly reduced. Opt for passionate work. Lukewarm work will not really sustain you.

If I had to tease out the key motivator that fuels the artist's journey, it would be passion. Passion creates and restores mental energy. Many people feel mentally tired a lot of the time and don't realize that nothing creates mental energy or restores it when it has drained away better than love, enthusiasm, and curiosity.

If you're a painter, just consider what looking at and being with paintings you love does to you — those paintings wake you right up. If you're sleepwalking through your art career, not quite getting things done, not quite feeling motivated, not quite feeling like tackling the projects that you claim interest you, it may well be that you've lost love for your own ideas — or maybe that you never fell in love with them in the first place.

Nor would that be very surprising. We have enough doubts about our right to create, the importance of creating, the general goodness of our work, and the goodness of the specific project (we say) we are working on, that we often dislike our projects more than we like them. Creating is hard, and what that means is that every day we may find our project hard — and it is difficult to love something that only presents us with problems.

So it's not surprising that we may not be bringing much love or passion to our creative efforts or our career in the arts. Since that love may not come naturally or may evaporate all too easily in the face of difficulties, you must learn how to kindle passion — and how to rekindle it when it vanishes.

It might sound as if I'm talking about how to bring fire back into a marriage, and in a way I am. In a dull, stressful marriage, very little that's lively or beautiful is going on. If you're in a dull, stressful relationship with your art, you can bet that very little that's lively or beautiful is going on there. So let's begin by looking at some ways to rekindle that passion.

1. *Get obsessed.* I've written extensively about the idea of "productive obsessions" in my book *Brainstorm* and recommend that book to you. The word *obsession* got

co-opted by the mental health industry and turned into a negative by definition. When you define *obsessions* as "intrusive, unwanted thoughts," then naturally all obsessions seem negative. But not every repetitive thought is unwanted or intrusive — some are exactly the thoughts we *want*. One way to fall back in love with your work is to allow yourself to obsess about it — to really bite into it, to really think about it, and to pay real, obsessive attention to it.

2. *Be a little more impetuous.* You may be living in a careful, controlled, and contained way to ensure that you are taking care of all your responsibilities and getting the items checked off your perpetual to-do list. That way of living can be entirely appropriate, but it pretty much bars the door on impetuosity. Try being more impetuous both with your art and with your art career. Impetuously get up from whatever you are doing and go write. Impetuously drop a gallery owner in London an email that introduces you. Write a song out of the blue. In the family of words that includes *loving* and *passionate, impetuous* is a vital one.

3. *Accept that you have appetites.* We rein in our appetites for all sorts of reasons: so that we don't gain too much weight, so that we don't have affairs and betray our mate, so that we don't drive too fast and get too many speeding tickets, and so on. We all have these appetites, and creative people tend to have even bigger appetites than most, which is why addiction is such a big problem in the arts. But when we try to rein in these appetites, as an unintended consequence we also rein in our appetite to create. Rather than reining in all your appetites, just rein in those that produce negative consequences. Let yourself be really hungry when it comes both to your creating and to your art career.

4. *Be ambitious.* Sometimes we sell ourselves on the idea that it is unseemly to have ambitions and that ambitiousness is a manifestation of narcissism or pride. It is really nothing of the kind. To have ambitions is really just to have desires, to have passions. It is perfectly proper to have desires and passions and to want things like bestsellers, or gallery shows, or articles written about you, or anything of that sort. Try to free yourself from the idea that there is something wrong with feeling and being ambitious, since those ambitions are really just manifestations of desire — and desire is a good thing!

5. *Feel devoted to your work.* The late Luciano Pavarotti said something once that I like to repeat: "People think I'm disciplined. It's not discipline, it's devotion, and there's a great difference." There is. We are in a completely different relationship with our art when we feel devoted to it as opposed to when we feel it is something we should be doing. If you have never felt really devoted to anything, you may want to locate that feeling in your being and to start treating your art as an object of your devotion.

6. *Opt for intensity and even exhaustion.* One of the ways we honor our pledge to make personal meaning is to do the work required of us, even if that effort exhausts us. If it exhausts us, we rest, but we do not let the fear of exhaustion prevent us from making our meaning.

You might start painting at sunrise and go until midnight, getting tired, confused, anxious, frayed, sad, and whatever else befalls you as you struggle to create. When, after many hours of doing battle, you can't muster another thought or another brushstroke, you can scream, cry, feed the cat, do anything you like, but do not even think about throwing in the towel. Try to live that intensely. Exhaust yourself in the service of your work, and then reward yourself, at the very least with the compliment "I worked hard, I didn't fall apart, and I'm proud of my efforts."

7. *Understand the power of our cultural and societal injunctions against passion.* Those injunctions can easily stop you from expressing the passion you feel. We are a very buttoned-down, unexpressive, don't-let-your-emotions-show kind of culture, and everyone is in that cultural trance. It can feel very hard to go against the grain and act passionately in the service of your ideas and projects. If you know that you are somehow inhibited by cultural messages and by the demand not to look conspicuous, think through what you can do to shed that cultural straitjacket.

8. *Remember that passion isn't unseemly.* We have to get it out of our heads that being passionate about our work, being obsessed with our work, or being in love with our work is unseemly. If we are holding some mental injunction against passion or some internal lack of permission to be passionate, that judgment will severely restrict our ability to create.

9. *Remember that passion isn't a given.* You have to bring the passion — it won't appear just because you showed up at the canvas or the computer screen. You know how often you show up and nothing exciting, invigorating, or passionate happens. The mere getting there isn't enough. You need to bring some enthusiasm, love, and passion with you, which you do by actively falling back in love with your project, by investing meaning in your project, and by thinking thoughts that serve you, in this instance loving thoughts.

10. *Remember that passion isn't optional.* To repeat the main point here, we have very little mental energy for something that bores us, for something that barely interests us, for something whose difficulty outweighs

its desirability. If we think of our work as difficult and believe we need a white-knuckled discipline to get to it, then we probably won't get to it. If, instead, we think of our work as difficult *and* as something we love and to which we are devoted, then we probably will get to it. Love makes all the difference in the world.

Passion and Voice

A logical — and vital — relationship exists between passion and voice. It is very hard to be passionate about what you're doing if you haven't found your voice as an artist. Imagine being forced to sing an octave too high or an octave too low, straining to hit notes that you can't really hit and that aren't natural to you. It would be very hard to be passionate about singing in that situation.

It is exactly like that with respect to whatever art you are creating. Whether you have been forced by circumstance not to create in your own voice, or whether you've avoided creating in your own voice for psychological reasons, the result will be a tremendous lack of passion for what you're doing. Creating in your authentic voice produces and sustains passion.

With that in mind, here are ten tips for finding or reclaiming your voice. They are framed in terms of visual art, so if you are not a visual artist you will need to translate them so that they make sense for your art discipline.

1. *Detach from your current visual library.* A very common problem, and almost always an unconscious one, is the need an artist feels to make his work look like something he holds as "good art" or "real art" — very often old master art. Because he possesses an internal library of the successful artworks of well-known artists, without quite realizing that he is doing it, he aims his art in the direction of those successes. It is vital

that an artist detach from that visual library — extinguish it, as it were — so that his own imagery has a chance to appear.

2. *Try not to rest on skills and talent.* Maybe you excel at producing dynamic-looking cats or turning a patch of yellow into a convincing sun. That you have these talents doesn't mean that you ought to be producing lifelike cats or brilliant suns. Your strongest subject matter and style choices depend on what you want to say rather than on what you are good at producing. By all means, parlay your skills and talents — but don't rely on them so completely that you effectively silence yourself.

3. *Allow risk-taking to feel risky.* Very often the personal work you want to do feels risky. Intellectually, you may find a way to convince yourself that the risk is worth taking — but when you try to take the risk, you balk because you suddenly feel anxiety welling up. Remember that a risk is likely to *feel risky*. Get ready for that reality by practicing and *owning* one or two robust anxiety-management strategies (more than a score of them are described in my book *Mastering Creative Anxiety*).

4. *Complete projects for the sake of making progress.* When you make new work that you think aims you in the direction of your genuine voice, try to complete that work rather than stopping midway because "it doesn't look right" or "it isn't working out." You will make more progress if you push through those feelings, complete things, and only *then* appraise them. It is natural for work that is a stretch and new to you to provoke all sorts of uncomfortable feelings as you attempt it. Help yourself tolerate those feelings by reminding yourself that finishing is a key to progress.

5. *Think at least a little bit about positioning.* You may

want to develop your voice independent of art trends and say exactly what you want to say in exactly the way you want to say it. On the other hand, it may serve you to take an interest in what's going on and make strategic decisions about how you want to position yourself vis-à-vis the world of galleries, collectors, exhibitions, auctions, movements, and so on. It isn't so much that one way is right and the other is wrong but rather that some marriage of the two, if you can pull it off, may serve you best: a marriage, that is, of marketplace strategizing and of intensely personal work that allows you to speak passionately in your own voice.

6. *Try to articulate what you're attempting.* Artists are often of two minds as to whether they want to describe what they are attempting. Paraphrasing a visual experience into a verbal artist's statement often feels unconvincing and beside the point. On the other hand, it can prove quite useful to announce to yourself what you hope to accomplish with your new work. By trying to put your next efforts into words, you may clarify your intentions and as a consequence more strongly value your efforts. The better you can describe what you are doing, the better you may understand your artistic voice — and the more passionate you can be in talking about your work.

7. *Try not to repeat yourself.* Repeating successful work has a way of reducing anxiety and can bring financial rewards as well. But it may also prevent us from moving forward and discovering what we hope to say. A balance to strike might be to do a certain amount of repeat work, for the sake of calmness and for the sake of your bank account, and to also add new work to your agenda. If you keep repeating yourself, it will prove very hard to remain passionate about your work.

8. *Revisit your earliest passions.* Life has a way of causing us to forget where our genuine passions reside. You may have spent decades in a big city and completely forgotten how much the desert means to you. You may have been so busy painting and parenting that your burning passion for creating a series of cityscapes fell off the map somewhere along the line. Finding your voice may involve something as simple and straightforward as making a list of your loves and starring the ones that still energize you. This is one of the simplest and smartest ways to discover what you are passionate about and what you want to say.

9. *Think about integrating your different styles.* Maybe you make two sorts of art, abstract relief paintings and realistic flat paintings. This division may have occurred at some point when, perhaps without consciously thinking the matter through, you decided that the one painting style allowed you to do something that the other didn't. It may pay you to revisit this question today and see if the two styles can be integrated into some third style that allows the best of both current styles to come together. Whatever you discover from that investigation — whether it's to move forward in a new way or to recommit to your current methods — you will have helped yourself better understand your artistic intentions. A lot of new passion can arise from these efforts at integration.

10. *Accept never-before-seen results.* It can feel odd to speak in your own voice and then not recognize the results. Because what you've created may be genuinely new — and completely new to you — it may look like nothing you've ever seen before. That can prove disconcerting! Don't rush to judge it as too odd, a mess or a mistake, or not what you'd intended. Give it some time to grow

on you and speak to you. Your voice may sound unfamiliar to you if you've never heard it before!

Remember: one of the keys to maintaining passion and enthusiasm for your work is finding your own voice and speaking in it.

Passion, Appetite, and Addiction

As noted earlier, creative people have passions and appetites — and that makes them prone to addiction.

If you're having trouble with some substance or behavior, the best plan is to create a recovery program for yourself — which simply means a plan for taking your problem seriously. In my book *Creative Recovery*, coauthored with addiction specialist Dr. Susan Raeburn, I describe a recovery program specially suited for artists. If you suspect that addiction may be a problem for you, please consider adopting the program described in that book.

Here let me provide just a few headlines to help you picture what dealing with your addiction would look like, and the steps you would need to take:

1. *Think about the consequences of your using.* You want a clear picture of what substances you are using or what behaviors you're engaging in, when you are using, what negative consequences occur because of your use, and so on. You want to apply your awareness to your addictive tendencies and get clarity about that picture.

2. *Consider any special "creative person" risks that make you especially vulnerable to addiction.* What in your personality — your appetites, the way you get existentially sad, the way you rev yourself up and shoot adrenaline into your system — puts you at risk for addiction?

3. *Also consider any special "creative life" risks that particularly trouble you.* Do rejection letters get under your skin so deeply that you're inclined to use? Is your band environment so drug-rich that it's hard not to participate? You want to identify the risks that are going to jeopardize your recovery.

4. *Create a picture of your recovery tasks.* What is your recovery program going to look like? Will you join a 12-step group, join a secular version of a 12-step group, or work your recovery on your own — and if you work it on your own, what will your plan look like? How will you create it, and what steps and tasks will it include?

5. *Study the recovery process.* You want a clear understanding that it is a process and not an event, that you are not out of the woods if after a year you haven't had a drink or a gambling escapade, that there will likely be slipups and lapses and that they aren't reasons to quit your program. You want to get a clear picture of what the recovery process is going to look like.

6. *Think through the ideas of surrender and acceptance.* You want to understand that you are admitting that you have not been in control of your use, that you are surrendering to that truth, and that you accept that you must pay real attention to your recovery needs. You are surrendering to a new way of life and accepting that new way of life, one in which your recovery program comes first.

7. *Identify any triggers, including any self-talk triggers, that tend to push you in the direction of using.* Is receiving a rejection email a trigger? Is an upcoming studio visit a trigger? Is saying to yourself "I have no chance" a trigger? You want to know what sorts of things trigger your desire to use — and you want to know what

you are going to do when you encounter one of those triggers.

8. *Get a sense of the role creative effort plays in your recovery program.* In the beginning you may have to modulate your ambitions and your creative efforts so as not to jeopardize your recovery; at the same time, you do want to include creating in your recovery program. In other words, you want to learn how to balance your need for creating with the risks associated with creating.

It is odd and disconcerting that an abundance of life energy can put us at risk for addiction. Yet that is exactly the case. We want to be passionate about our creating and passionate about our marketing efforts, but we also want to monitor the ways that our passions play out negatively, whether it's through a sexual addiction, a drug addiction, or, as in the following vignette, a shopping addiction.

Soothing Shopping

Alison wrote romances. She'd written three, one of which had been published. It did nicely, and the door to further successes seemed to be open — or at least ajar. But she was taking too long writing her current book, far too long, and the people who had been waiting for it — her agent and her editor — had given up. Alison kept in touch with them and kept offering explanations for her tardiness — explanations that in the beginning had been met with sympathy and that now were met with grudging, perfunctory replies.

"What's going on?" I asked.

She named several problems. She'd gotten it into her head that she had to top her published book, but she didn't know what that really meant. She didn't know the setting for her current romance very well and had spent a lot of time —

maybe too much time — researching it. The plot wasn't really "there." There wasn't much chemistry between the man and the woman. On the home front, there was a lot of chaos — her husband wasn't bringing in as much money as he used to, which made everything tight, and which made it necessary for her to work a part-time job. The kids had their problems. The house needed repairs, which they had decided to try to do themselves… She continued on for a while explaining her situation.

"And?" I asked when she'd finished. I felt that there was something else.

"And I buy things all day long!" she exclaimed. "It's completely out of control."

"Tell me about that."

She heaved a big sigh. "Sometimes I think that my goal is to keep us poor, so that I have to work, which keeps me from writing and keeps me from having to deal with agents and editors and all that. But I don't really think that's my nefarious plan. It's just…soothing to shop. It gives me pleasure. It's where I put my energy and my passion. I don't know that anything else gives me that much pleasure. I hate it when the things arrive; I hate it when I look at our finances; but when I'm shopping, I'm happy. It's like a magic spell."

"How many hours a day does that steal?"

"You could put it that way. Or you could say, how many hours of pleasure a day does it bring?" She smiled a small smile. "Maybe four hours a day. Maybe that's conservative. Maybe it's a lot more. Considering how much looking I do, I don't really buy that much!"

"You said it beautifully. It's the way you soothe yourself. The way you deal with your anxiety. And maybe even the place where you put a lot of your natural passion. That would be no problem — except that it sounds like you've crossed the line."

"I've crossed the line. I used to write, shop online a little,

THE PASSION KEY

55

write, reward myself with some more shopping — now it's just the shopping."

I nodded. "So. Here's the plan. This book needs to get finished — and be good. How much of it is done?"

"Maybe twenty thousand words. But I don't know if they're worth saving."

"Right. So let's start there. Let's get those twenty thousand words off to some readers. You have folks you use?"

She nodded. "I do. There are several women — we read and critique one another's work. We support one another."

"Right. Bite the bullet and get your partial off to three or four of them. Let's see what they think."

"Okay."

"How long will it take them to get back to you?"

"It'll take me a week to get the partial together — I need to read it one more time — then, maybe two weeks? Three weeks?"

"Okay! Do you want to start writing right away, or do you want to wait and hear what they have to say?"

"I'd like to wait —"

"Okay. Then we have a month to start dealing with this addiction."

She took the word in. "You'd say it's a real addiction?"

"You've lost control?"

She nodded.

"Real enough, then," I said.

"Actually," she said, visibly relaxing, "I'm glad to give it that big a name. With a smaller name, I just wasn't going to tackle it. Calling it an addiction — that sounds serious. It got my attention."

I smiled. "That's what we want. Let me outline what a recovery program looks like."

I spent the next ten minutes explaining what she was going to need to do. She would stop her online shopping completely. She would create other, healthier self-care and soothing strategies. She would check with her HMO to see if they offered any classes or groups geared specifically to a shopping addiction. If they didn't, she would look into the 12-step world or some other group support. She would begin to say out loud, "I have a shopping addiction" and remind herself that she was taking the problem seriously. She would reduce contact with her shopping buddies and create a set of strategies to employ when the shopping fever hit. Most of all, she would surrender to the fact that shopping had crossed over from being a passion to a problem. Shopping could no longer be her lover.

"I can't ever shop again?" she asked woefully. "It's like alcohol?"

"The starting place is to stop and to enter recovery. We can get appropriate shopping back on the table at some point — but that's putting the cart before the horse. Now the job is recovering. Deal?"

She nodded.

"But this won't make the writing easier," I said. "It may even make it harder at first, given that you may be agitated and craving some way to soothe yourself. So we need a very simple plan for the writing, an exceptionally simple plan. You will just show up."

She thought about that.

"Once you resume the romance, after you hear back from your readers, your goal will be to just show up, every day or almost every day, at your computer. All right?"

"All right," she said. "And thanks a lot. Can I buy you anything?"

That was good for a laugh — although hers wasn't very hearty.

In Honor of Passionate Creation

Our desire to create a world is like the energy that causes strings to vibrate and matter to come together. The instant our desire stops, our world-building grinds to a halt. The instant our desire returns, we find ourselves at play again in the fields of art. Focus on desire, then! When your project stalls, when you fear that you have no ideas, when you can't open the studio door, cry out for desire — *demand* desire!

For every stage of the art-making process, an excellent solution to the problems that arise is the rekindling of desire. If the problem is that a corner of your current canvas is dull, you rekindle your desire to breathe life into it. If the problem is that it is time to write your artist statement and the absurdity of that task demoralizes you, you rekindle your desire to let the world know about your work. Whatever the problem is, *lead with passion*. If you can flip the passion switch and feel that burst of energy rise within you, the problem that a moment before looked insurmountable will have shrunk to something laughably modest.

Here, then, is a little creation ditty, our artist version of the Babylonian Genesis:

> *I am a world-builder.*
> *That isn't so easy.*
> *But I am a world-builder.*
> *Even with all my disabilities.*
> *I am a world-builder.*
> *Desire is the complete prescription.*
> *Whether I find myself at the beginning of a work of art, in*
> *   the middle, or near its completion.*
> *Without desire I am done.*
> *So every day I rekindle my desire. Somehow!*

Cadmium Red

Jack worked in grays. His skies were gray; his fields were gray; everything he produced felt like a dark day in winter. Clouds hanging low, a storm coming…his paintings made you want to turn up the heat and fix a pot of tea.

I sat waiting. Jack couldn't quite explain why he had come to see me. In his first email he'd said, "I'd love some coaching on my issues." That hadn't told me much! When I asked him to preview those issues, he didn't reply until the morning of our appointment, and then only to say, "I'm running late today — I'll tell you in person." Now we were in person — and he was still having trouble.

"I'm not exactly sure why I'm here," he said.

I nodded.

"My wife's read some of your books. She suggested I see you."

I laughed. "Not a good sign! It's better when my clients actually want to see me!"

"No, no," he said quickly, "I do want to see you. It's just…I can't find a way into my issues. I don't know what's bothering me. I love to go to the studio. I don't mind my day job — I do consulting work, and it isn't very taxing. And it pays well. I've set up my life pretty well for an artist. My wife and I are good — our children are good…" He trailed off.

"Your life sounds very nice, very pleasant."

He glanced at me. "I think you're saying something."

I shrugged. "I've looked at your paintings on your website. I can see them in an English country house, a horse-and-hound kind of estate, with roaring fires and your all-gray paintings fitting in perfectly."

"I spent two years in England, painting," he said. "I lived not far from Kenwood House, in Hampstead. I went there every few days — the Rembrandts, the early Turners —"

"Before Turner was Turner," I said.

That woke him up. "Before Turner was Turner?"

"I've seen those Turners. Conventional, dark, very old master, like Van Gogh's early work, that Dutch palette, that darkness, that moodiness, as if color hadn't been invented yet."

"That's what I've always aspired to being. An old master."

"Not a bad thing, I'm sure." I paused. "Or is it?"

"Well, I've never thought that passion was such a good thing. My parents were dramatic and explosive. I wanted... calmness. My paintings are intentionally quiet."

"Yes."

"That's worked for me."

I waited.

"But," he continued, "there's certainly a line to walk between calmness and...death. To ensure my sanity, I've probably become a little dead."

I nodded. "Let me ask you a question."

"Yes?"

"Do you love any one color more than the other colors?"

He replied instantly. "Yes! I love red. Cadmium red. Soutine's red."

"And you're prohibited from using it because of your safety needs? It feels too dangerous to use cadmium red?"

He thought about that and grew agitated. "I don't know what I would paint if I started using color. Not circle paintings! Not stripe paintings! There are a million things that don't interest me. Not a photo-realist red lollipop, not grotesque torsos."

I smiled. "You don't respect anything done in the past one hundred and fifty years of paintings?"

"No, of course I do. It's just —"

"The orderliness of formal art matched your desire for orderliness. I'll bet you a nickel that you like things in order. I bet your paints and your socks are in perfect order. But there's a cost to managing your anxiety that way. It may be a cost that you are entirely willing to pay. The cost is that you've prevented yourself from using color. You've made a deal with yourself — or with the devil — no passion, no problems."

He made no reply. Downcast, he said, "Of course that

applies to everything. To the way I feel uncomfortable if I pour myself more than four ounces of wine…"

"Yes. You've done a gorgeous job of being careful, really a beautiful job. It might be a big mistake to upset that apple-cart. You might get some red paintings out of it — but who knows what else might happen."

He thought about that for a long time. Finally he spoke. "It's all well and good to say to yourself, 'Take a risk.' But if it's a real risk…There was a weekend in Amsterdam — I almost threw over my whole life just because I met a woman and it was Amsterdam and I could see exactly how it would play out, the passion part and the abyss. Fortunately nothing happened. It would have been a mistake."

"Red would be that kind of mistake?"

He shook his head speculatively. "I don't know."

We sat in silence. Taking a risk is not the answer to every problem. Sometimes the life we've constructed, even if it falls short of the ideal, suits us better than some riskier alternative. Jack mulled the matter over.

"What if I put a little red in my landscapes?" he finally said.

I laughed. "A careful solution! Do you think that might work?"

"I think that I'd rather try that than throw over my paint-ing style and my subject matter for the sake of some idealized notion of passion. I'd really rather not create tempests and dramas. Just a little red —"

"Just a little red but a lot of passion?" I asked.

He thought about that. "I can feel how that might work. 'A little red but a lot of passion.' That has a good ring to it."

I smiled. "Be careful about opening that door a crack. You might move all the way from *Potato Eaters* to *Sunflowers!*"

"Careful is my middle name," Jack replied. "I suspect you won't even be able to see the red!"

"To begin with."

"Yes, well, to begin with," he agreed. "I guess we'll have to see how dangerous a little cadmium red really is!"

In Praise and Pursuit of Passion

Passion fuels an artist's journey. If you are to succeed as an artist, you must bring the passion. Try answering the following questions:

- Are you passionate enough about your creative work?
- What causes you to lose passion for your creative work?
- How do you sustain passion for your creative projects?
- What do you see as the difference between passion and mere interest?
- What are your thoughts on the kindling and rekindling of desire?

You will not be able to muster passion all the time. Human beings are not built to be perpetual volcanoes. You may go for days just forcing yourself to show up at your creative work. That forcing and that showing up are honorable and necessary. At the same time, do try to locate and kindle your passion. You don't need it, and you can't have it, every day, but you do need it as your core orientation. Something in you must ignite at least some of the time if your work is to feel alive and if *you* are to feel alive.

Chapter 4

THE FREEDOM KEY

Do you make use of your freedom to nurture, support, and create your best life in the arts?

We are free in certain senses and not free in others. Understanding this truth is one face of wisdom. There is almost nothing that we are free to control. By the same token there is almost nothing that we aren't free to influence. The difference between control and influence is vital. The more you feel that you control nothing, the sadder and more passive you become. The more you see it as your job to exert the influence that is yours to exert, the more likely you are to spend your days actively making meaning.

Let's take a simple example. Say that you want the book you've written to be picked up by a major publisher. You are not free to make that happen — you can't control that at all. But you are completely free to *try* to make that happen, to *keep trying* to make that happen, and to profoundly influence the process by creating something that's wanted, by properly building your platform, by networking in the right ways, and so on.

You may want more freedom than that, a more pervasive, larger freedom to make things happen in exactly the ways that you want them to happen. That freedom you don't possess. What you do possess is the freedom to positively influence the process. If you give up *that* freedom, it is *you* who is giving it up and no one else. To create your best life in the arts, you must figure out what freedom you *do* possess and then make powerful and consistent use of that freedom.

Even in areas where we are potentially free to influence the process, we often give that freedom away. This is one of our worst habits. When we give away the freedom we do possess, we feel weak and powerless, we feel disappointed in our efforts; it is as if we are just going through the motions. Do not give away the limited freedom that you do possess! Don't pass up calling someone who might be helpful because you are feeling shy or anxious or because you feel stubbornly resentful that you need help. Don't retreat from the marketplace because someone criticizes you. It is our job to focus on the ways in which we are free. It is our job to remind ourselves of all our freedoms — our freedom to try, our freedom to get out of our own way, our freedom to say what we mean, our freedom to advocate for ourselves.

There are many different sorts of freedom — there's political freedom, economic freedom, and so on. I am focusing on psychological freedom — the freedom, for example, to think thoughts that serve you, to advocate for yourself, to resolve simmering internal conflicts; on societal freedom — the freedom not to live by society's dictates but to carve out your own path and your own destiny; and on what we might call career freedom — that is, the freedom to try to succeed in the marketplace. There are many arenas in life in which we must try to maintain our freedom, and these three — social freedom, psychological freedom, and career freedom — are of paramount importance to artists.

Just asking ourselves questions about where we are free and where we are not increases our freedom. If you ask yourself, "What gets in the way of my being psychologically free?," "What gets in the way of my acting freely in society?," and "What gets in the way of my asserting my freedom in the marketplace?," you immediately begin to regain your freedom. The moment you begin asking yourself, "Where did these shackles come from?," you begin to notice those shackles, and you begin to want to do something about them.

Both our society and we ourselves pressure us to relinquish our freedom. The pressures that society applies on us to be conventional and unfree — let's call that social censorship — and the pressure we apply on ourselves not to take risks, not to speak our mind, and so on — let's call that self-censorship — are powerful inhibiting factors in a creative person's life.

Let's take a simple example in each category. You probably do not feel particularly free to stop in a supermarket aisle while you're shopping and work on a poem that's just come to you — even though you are perfectly free to do that. Who stole that freedom from you? Who made it hard, verging on impossible, for you to work like the artist you are in a conspicuous place like a busy supermarket?

That's a simple example of how we let society make us unfree. Here's a simple example of self-censorship. How many times have you come up against a subject-matter choice in your art that you know would be interesting and maybe even brilliant to examine, but somewhere inside you felt that it was better left unexamined? That is self-censorship in action. We desire to tackle some dangerous, fascinating subject — and we ourselves shut that desire down. In such ways we reduce our own freedom.

We are pressured into censoring ourselves in public and

private all the time by unseen forces, and we must fight back against these pressures. We must use the freedom available to us and the personality available to us if we are to manifest the freedom that we do possess and if we are to create a life in the arts that we truly desire rather than one built to feel safe.

People flee freedom all the time. Many people actively hate freedom as an idea. There is a large literature on authoritarian submission — that is, on the personality profile of the person who passionately prefers tyranny to freedom. But people flee from freedom in many other ways, in addition to handing their freedom off to tyrants. Many people let their safety needs trump their freedom needs and live a restricted life based on the concept of safety. Others — and this is a real problem for artists — substitute habitual thinking for fresh, free, in-the-moment thinking so as not to rock their world with the freedom of fresh thought. People flee from freedom all the time — and artists flee from freedom in their own special ways. Do not be that kind of artist!

Artists rarely recognize that a flight from freedom is preventing them from doing their deepest, most interesting, most challenging work. For example, they equate "having an idea" with "freely thinking about." Many creative people settle on an idea for a creative piece — a novel, a film, a painting, and so on — without ever thinking through what they would really like to tackle. They get it into their heads, for example, that it "might be interesting" to paint pumpkins in purple, but they never quite examine what painting deeply, meaningfully, and freely might mean to them. This settling on a reasonable idea is one of the most common ways that creative people flee freedom, and it occurs because they do not understand that their very freedom hangs in the balance when they choose their subject matter.

It is one thing when someone else prevents you from saying what's on your mind and in your heart and quite another when you yourself avoid your deepest — that is, your freest —

work. To repeat this point: artists rarely recognize that when they are choosing a creative project to work on, they are in the territory of freedom. It is part of an artist's job description to become an expert on freedom. That is, it is *your* job!

Free to Prove the Exception

Most people are not able to create a successful life in the arts. The problems are Darwinian and concern supply and demand. There aren't enough slices of the pie for all the people who want to act, dance, write, paint, sing, and direct. Whether it is one person in a hundred who makes it in your discipline or one in ten thousand, you want to be that one. You are free to try to prove the exception and be that one.

Of course you may simply get lucky and become that one: maybe the gods of whimsy smile down on you; maybe you get discovered through some quirky accident; maybe you have all the right connections. All those things can and do happen. On the other hand, you may not want to bank on gods, luck, and connections. You may decide to exert your freedom and try your darnedest to prove the exception. Here are ten tips for doing just that:

1. *Understand why proving the exception is vital.* First, understand this point. There are many places in life where you might want to prove the rule and not the exception. In a certain kind of salaried government job where your main task is not to rock the boat, then not rocking the boat is exactly what you want to do if you hope to get along and succeed. In many situations you want to do exactly what everyone else is doing, for example, driving on the correct side of the road. In the arts, however, you do not want to be doing what everyone else is doing: you want to be doing both *more* and *different.*

2. *Understand how most artists operate.* If you intend to prove the exception, you will need to learn what is average or typical. Use the evidence of your eyes to distinguish between what most artists are doing and what successful artists are doing. What concrete differences do you notice between one group and the other? Are the successes of thriving artists more about their subject-matter choices, their technical merit, their marketing efforts, the stunts they pull, their assertiveness, or their sociability? What do you see? If you don't know how to gather this information, think about how you might gather it. If you can't gather it, then just use your common sense to answer the following basic, pivotal question: What helps a person succeed?

3. *Articulate the difference(s) between the "normal way" and the "exceptional way."* As you begin to understand what amounts to an average effort and what amounts to an exceptional effort, articulate what you are learning. Write out your own ten tips for proving the exception. Be able to say in a clear sentence how you mean to distinguish your efforts from customary ones. This might sound like "I am spending the next six months creating a powerful body of work, and then I am completely turning myself over to marketing that work with as much passion, pride, and smarts as I used when creating the work." Create your plan for proving the exception. Clearly identify what you will need to make your plan work.

4. *Step into the shoes of someone exceptional.* Once you've articulated your understanding of the differences between an average effort and an exceptional one, you will want to become the person capable of making such efforts. This may mean working on your shyness, your anxieties, your passivity, and your dislike

of self-promotion. If proving the exception requires that you do *x*, *y*, and *z*, you must become the person capable of doing *x*, *y*, and *z*. Rehearse being this new person. Set up real-world opportunities to be this new person. Maybe what you are doing is crafting a public persona, or maybe you are actually changing, but in either event you must become capable of the exceptional efforts required of you.

5. *Reach out.* One of your jobs is to learn how to send clear, concise, friendly, useful emails and other messages to the people who might be able to help you. There's no need to labor over such missives — they do not need to be elaborate works of art or skillful apologies for why you aren't further along in your career but rather simple announcements and requests in which you advocate for you and your work and use the freedom you possess, both technological and existential, to create success. Reach out to three people a day... to five people a day...to seven people a day. Reach out so that you're read and published, viewed and collected, heard and downloaded. Reach out regularly and continually.

6. *Follow through.* It is one thing to make a sensible plan — for your current novel, for your art-marketing efforts, for your financial stability — and another to follow through on all the steps required to turn any plan into a successful experience. You will come up against innumerable obstacles, external and internal, as you endeavor to follow through, from doubts and worries to unreturned emails and phone calls to technological glitches to rude, offhanded criticism to deals falling through to contracts not being honored. Persevere; follow through; keep at it! Following through is rather exceptional — most people start and then stop.

7. *Become really available.* You could act as if relating in

the marketplace is a tremendously burdensome thing and make yourself only grudgingly available — for meetings, for interviews, for audience contact — or you could invite such interactions, make dates for coffee, accept any and all invitations to speak or be interviewed, and otherwise become readily available. Become a recluse after you are famous, not before. Yes, you need studio time; yes, you need time for the rest of your life, including time for your day job and your loved ones; and yet you must still find the time and the wherewithal to make yourself really available. Much of your competition, primarily out of anxiety, will stubbornly refuse to do this — you are free to make yourself more available than them and in that way prove the exception.

8. *Create events and the occasional stunt.* Create events, such as shows you curate, readings you organize, concerts you hammer into existence, and social media extravaganzas. Occasional stunts may also be necessary. A stunt is a splashy event created to produce publicity. It might be you shredding your unwanted paintings in a public place with the press alerted; it might be you attending your opening nude; it might be you marrying and divorcing another artist in a ceremony the two of you design to advertise your "marriage doesn't work" suite of paintings. Most artists hate stunts. It is nevertheless worth your while to calmly think through your relationship to stunts. Who knows? You may actually have a stunt or two up your sleeve that you would enjoy dropping on an unsuspecting public!

9. *Angle for bigger outcomes.* Keep your eyes peeled for bigger outcomes from the marketing and promoting work that you do. Convince a friendly gallery owner not to hang just one or two of your paintings but to

give you a whole show. Use your rhetorical skills and powers of persuasion to angle for that bigger outcome. Ask a friendly collector not only to take a look at your new body of work but also to throw an event in support of it. Use your charm and smarts to angle for this bigger outcome. Each time you think about attempting something, ask yourself, "What bigger outcome could I angle for with exactly the same amount of effort?"

10. *Think globally.* It is wonderful to be represented by the gallery down the street, but it is unlikely, verging on impossible, that you can prove the exception if your field of vision is limited to your immediate neighborhood. What if the galleries most likely to be interested in you are scattered all over the world? Then you must find them and reach out to them. It is excellent to fashion and maintain local relationships, but to prove the exception, you will need to make the world your oyster. Because of contemporary technology this has never been easier; and while everyone is using that technology as a matter of course, you can prove the exception by taking that technological capability and harnessing it to build your reputation and your best life in the arts.

Free to Make Meaning

Meaning is a modern problem, and I've written extensively in books such as *The Van Gogh Blues*, *Coaching the Artist Within*, *Rethinking Depression*, and many others about how it affects creative people. I don't want to repeat myself here. Rather, let me present this headline: You are free to make meaning, and you are obliged to do so. In *Rethinking Depression* I provide a complete existential program for doing just that, and I recommend that you read it as a supplement to this discussion.

Here I want to provide one simple, straightforward technique for making use of the freedom you possess to create the meaning you need. It is the idea of a morning meaning check-in where, first thing each day and before your "real day" starts, you envision your day and decide where you will make your daily meaning investments. This morning meaning check-in, which takes a minute or two at most, reminds you of your intentions, focuses your mind, increases your resolve, and helps you live more mindfully and more powerfully.

The existentialists say that we are contingent — that we are born into a certain family, born into a certain social class, alive at a time of war or of peace, and so on. These are our contingencies, our facts of existence. But we are also free — free to adopt our basic attitudes, free to create, free to stand up and be counted. It is this latter freedom that you must not shirk. Yes, you are contingent in all sorts of binding and troublesome ways. You have those anxiety attacks. You have those unpaid bills. All that is real and true. But you are also free to live heroically, to make yourself proud, and to create your own meaning. Your morning meaning check-in is an aid in this.

Consider the experience of a client of mine named Barbara:

"I've been religiously doing the morning practice, and it's made a huge difference in my life. With each day's work building on previous days', I've pulled further out of acute depression.

"Morning practice was a natural for me as I'd been doing morning pages for about fifteen years after reading Julia Cameron's *The Artist's Way*. The tools that I set up in interpreting the morning practice instructions are a spiral notebook journal to use each morning to briefly write any thoughts that I wake up with (ideas, issues, dreams) and to write the meaningful activities I plan for the day.

"I also keep a monthly calendar page with squares large enough to write daily meaning activities I accomplished from the day before. The calendar provides an ongoing and cumulative record of the meaningful activities I actually managed to accomplish.

"In the journal, as I complete a meaning activity for the day, I put a broad red check mark beside it and the amount of time I spent on it (if that's important). On the monthly calendar I write a Post-it note with my 'productive obsession' and my three main, ongoing goals. I transfer those Post-its from month to month. I make the same Post-its to put before me on the desk and computer.

"At first I was confused about daily meaningful activities. There are things I have to do and things I want to do that have meaning. I determined I'd try to get in one to two hours of more meaningful activities daily. Then it evolved into not concerning myself with meeting the one to two hours of meaningful activities. I mulled this over and determined that I'm the one who says whether something is meaningful. So 'have tos' and 'want tos' both have meaning when I list and evaluate activities each day.

"As was promised, this morning practice takes only a few minutes each day (unless I write longer in the journal). So very important is the basic structure and routine, which is what I needed and which I haven't rebelled against, as I have throughout my life when I felt too boxed in. There is a logic and a spaciousness to this morning meaning practice that really works for me."

There are an infinite number of ways in which you are not free: you are not free to demand of an editor that she publish you; you are not free to solve a scientific problem if it isn't solvable; you are not free to make people buy your watercolors. But against all that are the ways in which you are free: free to make a daily effort in support of your creative life, free to make mistakes and messes in the service of your lifelong apprenticeship, free to aim for excellence. Use the freedom you have to make the meaning you require.

Free to Be Imperfect

Not so long ago I got an email from a painter in Rhode Island. She wrote, "I'm a perfectionist and I want my artwork to be perfect. Sometimes this prevents me from getting started on a new project or from finishing the one I'm working on. I think to myself, 'If it's not going to be the best, why bother to do it? How do I move past these feelings?'"

One way is to move from a purely intellectual understanding that messes are part of the creative process to a visceral understanding of that truth. As an intellectual matter, every artist knows that some percentage of her work will prove less than stellar, especially if she is taking risks with subject matter or technique. But far too many creative and would-be creative people have a lot of difficulty accepting that obvious truth.

Do you understand in your heart that messes and mistakes are not only okay but also part and parcel of the creative process and even crucial to the process? Of course they are not the goal — the goal is excellent work. But they are as integral to the process as falling down is to the process of learning to walk. An infant would never think, "I will not walk until I can walk perfectly." Only adults think such unhappy, paralyzing thoughts!

If an infant wants to get from where she is to the toy across the room, she will crawl, walk, tumble, or fly. She will do whatever it takes — because she really wants that rattle or ball! When an artist really wants to create, because she is excited by the prospect of turning her thoughts and feelings into tangible things, then perfection recedes as an issue. She is like the infant who wants the rattle: she becomes a beautiful vehicle of vitality and desire. First, gain permission in your heart of hearts to make mistakes and messes. Second, grow as excited about a creative project as a baby is about her rattle. Those are the twin ways to exorcise perfectionism.

When I begin a book — and I've written more than fifty

— I am excited to see what will emerge. Maybe something beautiful will appear on the first try; maybe the book will need two complete overhauls and three additional revisions; maybe it will never come to life and need to be abandoned. I am easy with all those outcomes, including the last. If I were not, I would be asking the creative process to be something that it cannot be: a guarantee that if I show up, excellent things will happen. The showing up is the main thing; the excellence, if it comes, is an added blessing.

Eliminate the word *perfection* from your vocabulary. Replace it with *freedom*. Cognitive therapists teach a useful three-step technique: First, learn to notice if and when the word *perfection* or some word or sentiment like it pops into your mind. Second, dispute it instantly by saying, "No! That's not a word I countenance!" Third, replace it with a more appropriate suggestion, for instance, "I am free, I am willing to struggle, and I will show up."

Giving Away Your Marketplace Freedom

The following are ten ways that creative and performing artists give away their freedom with respect to the art marketplace and their career. Please think about how often you give away your freedom in these ways — and pledge to stop doing it!

1. *By hiding out.* We are free to show up places, to learn from people, and to see what is going on, but out of anxiety or stubborn pride we give away this important freedom. You are also free *not* to hide out — that is your choice.

2. *By demonizing marketplace players.* It is easy and somehow comforting to mentally turn marketplace players into enemies, but we are also free *not* to take that easy route. It is our choice whether to lead with

disdain and wounded pride or to freely admit that we need these players, want them, and will do whatever we can to bring them over to our side. To repeat, we are free *not* to demonize marketplace players.

3. *By overinvesting in one plan or tactic.* We are free to step back and look at our plans and tactics objectively rather than to keep obsessing about the one plan or the one tactic in which we've invested everything. If you are obsessing about whether to serve cookies or muffins on open-studio day, that obsessing is preventing you from doing other things that would much better support your career. You are free *not* to obsess in such ways.

4. *By taking silence personally.* We send things out into the world, and then we wait. While we wait, all we hear is silence. We are free *not* to take that silence personally or to construe it as impending criticism or rejection. We are free to keep sending things out even as the silence mounts. We are free *not* to turn silence into a problem.

5. *By turning people who do not really matter to us into too much of a problem.* We are free not to care too much about or become too affected by difficult folks in the marketplace who do not directly affect us. If some gallery owner who is not showing our work takes crazy offense at the email we send him, we are free not to take his crazy offense to heart or to enter into his dramatic little world. We just smile and delete his rant. We are free *not* to care about people about whom we don't actually care.

6. *By failing to notice — and seize — opportunity.* We are free not to ignore the fact that someone we know knows someone who might be useful to us. Too often we feel embarrassed about reaching out to people who might be of use to us and therefore get in the habit of

not even noticing their existence. Countless clients of mine have failed to notice that a marketplace player has actually expressed interest in them or their work — somehow that information gets completely missed. You are free *not* to miss noticing the opportunities that arise and seizing them.

7. *By not persisting.* We are free to keep trying a given contact a dozen times, or we can give away that freedom by stopping the first time we are met with a lukewarm or negative response. If you improve a project, you are free to get back to anyone who passed on it the time before — unless you give up that freedom. If you receive a bit of attention, you are free to tell folks who have passed on your work before that you are better known or better received now — unless you give up that freedom. You are free to persist and even pester — unless you decide that you are not that free.

8. *By saying yes when it doesn't serve us or when we don't mean it.* We are free to say *no* to a time-consuming, low-paying gig, or we can give away that freedom and say yes just because we want to be seen as nice or helpful. We are free to say no to helping out with a labor-intensive project that provides us with next to nothing, or we can give away that freedom. We are free to think about whether a project really serves us — *or we can give away that freedom.*

9. *By taking long vacations from trying to move our career forward.* You are free to decide that you will not skip days and avoid the work necessary to give yourself a chance at a career. Taking days off is the same as giving away your freedom — your freedom to try, your freedom to make an effort, your freedom to give yourself a chance. You are free *not* to take extensive vacations from building your career.

10. *By throwing up our hands and exclaiming that we don't*

know what to do to move our career forward, that there are too many things to do to move our career forward, that we are too much of an outsider to move our career forward, that there are too few opportunities to move our career forward. In fact, you are free *not* to throw up your hands at marketplace difficulties. And that's exactly what you need to do: *not* throw up your hands at these difficulties.

The art marketplace is a hard enough place to navigate without your giving away your freedom to do normal, natural, and useful things on your own behalf. You may be embarrassed to do them; your pride may get in the way; your anxiety may get in the way. But all that is on your shoulders. The freedom is there. Make not giving it away your agenda.

Making Music

Annie had erected a wall that prevented her from making music. She could only play brilliantly. Every teacher and every reviewer said the same thing about her playing: it was technically perfect but had no soul. Sometimes they called her playing cold. Sometimes they called it mechanical. Sometimes they called it boring. They had different ways of saying the same thing: that she was a violin virtuoso who played notes and not music.

There is nothing the slightest bit rare about this. Mastering a musical instrument at the level needed to become a world-class soloist requires so much effort, especially if you lack some physical gift, that just getting the notes right is an immense accomplishment. It is one of the little jokes of the trickster gods to make it so hard to do the most beautiful things, like sing gorgeously in your upper register, that the difficulty overwhelms everything else. Many musicians are consumed by the difficulty of the thing they have chosen to do, spending a lifetime worrying about their shortcomings and the difficult passages ahead, and this worrying naturally kills off their joy.

Annie, a second-generation Korean American, came to see me reluctantly. She made appointments and canceled them. No doubt she presumed I had nothing to offer her, even though she enjoyed my books, as she mentioned in her first email to me. She understood about technical help and had worked with many violin teachers and medical specialists during her career. But how could a creativity coach help her with her playing? Perhaps it made very little sense to her.

After our brief pleasantries were over, at the beginning of our first real conversation I asked her, "What's on your mind? It wasn't so clear from your emails."

She didn't reply immediately. I wondered if she didn't know or if she preferred not to say. "I'm getting booked less," she finally said. "I had a career that was going up and now it's stagnating. New violinists are getting concerts that I think I should have gotten. I thought it was about my repertoire and maybe changing tastes and all that. Now I don't know."

"What do you now think it is?"

"I don't know."

"What are the two or three things it might be?"

"It might be that people don't like me. I don't have all the social graces. I'm not a networker. I'm uncomfortable around people, and they know it."

I nodded. "What else?"

"There are certain things that I'm obliged to play that I don't love to play, like the Tchaikovsky and the Mendelssohn violin concertos. I don't really like anything romantic or schmaltzy or anything that might be considered 'beautiful.' And people like those things."

"You say that people consider them beautiful. You don't?"

She made a face. "I listened to Oistrakh play the Tchaikovsky about a million times. Why? Not to hear how he handled it technically. Just to hear him play it. I am completely of two minds about a word like *beautiful*. On the one hand, it rubs me the wrong way. On the other…there's Oistrakh."

I let us be silent for a moment. The next question was not an easy one.

"Can you play beautifully?" I asked.

"People say that I can't," she replied. "In a way, I'm not even sure what they mean. I know they say that I'm a slave to the notes. But it doesn't feel that way to me. I feel like I'm making music. Sometimes I think they're just making it up, using that language as a way of saying that they prefer somebody else's playing to mine."

I nodded. "That could be. But tell me, do you feel free to drop notes and miss notes?"

She raised her head and stared at me. "I do not! Why would anyone feel free to do that? That's ridiculous! That's the first thing you need to get right. And…and…"

"Were you going to say, 'And the only thing'?"

She shrugged angrily.

"Many great musicians," I continued, "have said that if you demand that they play all the notes correctly, they can't also make music. You've heard that said?"

"Of course! But I've never taken that seriously. That's not what they mean! They mean, 'If I was a little off tonight, here's my excuse. I was making music.' It's just a kind of excuse! They don't mean it."

I waited. "What if they do mean it?" I asked.

"They can't!"

I let the silence be.

"You need to play the notes correctly," she said in a small voice.

"Of course." I paused. "But is that the music?"

"The music is notes in a score. I think about them, I figure them out, I play them, the strings vibrate and move the air — it's notes and sound waves."

"No heart?"

"I keep hearing that! 'No heart!' 'No heart!' I keep hearing that!" Tears came. "What am I supposed to do at this point? Go see the Wizard of Oz and get a heart? I'm really tired of hearing this!"

I smiled. "Well, I have a simple solution. Feel free to play in a heartfelt way, and the hell with the notes."

Annie stared at me. "Everybody would rip me apart if I did that."

"If you missed one or two notes in a concerto but brought tears to their eyes?"

That thought startled her. "If that were the trade-off…"

"Who knows? We're not talking about terrible playing. We're talking about free playing. Make a mental calculation. How many notes would it cost you to play more freely?"

She thought about that for a long time. I could see her playing in her mind's eye. Every once in a while she made a face — there was a missed note! Finally she sighed.

"I don't know. Just a few. Not that many."

"But you could sense the difference? Between playing correctly and playing freely?"

"In that split second I could. I don't know if I could with a violin in my hands. But of course I have to try it."

"Agreed."

"You know, I'm not really sure I know what we've been talking about."

I nodded. "Just think Oistrakh. You understood that perfectly."

She sighed. "Maybe. Let me see what happens when I try to play something."

"The Tchaikovsky." I laughed.

"No," she said, almost smiling. "But okay…maybe something beautiful."

Wondering about Freedom

Just caring about the issue of freedom is a great first step. The question "Am I really free to create what I want to create, or is something holding me back?" is a great one to wrestle with. Try to wonder about this rather than worry about it. Leading with worry will immediately raise your anxiety level and reduce your ability to think clearly. Just wonder lightly. "I wonder what I'd really like to paint next?" has a very different energy to it than "I'm really worried about what I'm going to paint next!"

Start to use the language of freedom. Begin to say things like "I'm interested in taking risks that support my freedom." By announcing that you are willing to risk, you remind yourself that freedom often comes at the price of feeling anxious. Check in with yourself on your psychological self-censorship by asking questions like "What don't I want to reveal?" and "How much is that energy of concealment restricting me?" The less willing you are to reveal your true thoughts and feelings, the less psychologically free you will be. And you want that freedom!

As an exercise, try adding a restriction and then taking it away. Doing this will give you a more refined sense of what freedom — and a lack of freedom — feel like. For example, try painting using only greens to see if a limited palette actually reduces your freedom or, paradoxically enough, increases your freedom, maybe by breaking you out of the habit of using so much red and blue. Dream up exercises for yourself that allow you to really feel and think through this issue of freedom.

Try answering the following questions:

- How do your circumstances render you less free?
- How does your history render you less free?
- How does your personality render you less free?
- How do your society and culture render you less free?
- And, most important, in what ways are you *still free*?

Chapter 5

THE STRESS KEY

Life produces stress, the artistic personality produces additional stress, creating produces even more stress, and living the artist's life is the topper! You must learn how to deal with all these stressors — and how to deal with them effectively. Let's begin by getting a clearer picture of what stress is and how it pertains to creative people in particular.

A stressor is *anything*, positive or negative, that makes a demand on us. Stress is our body's physical and psychological reaction to those demands — on the physical level, it is a buildup of chemicals that keeps increasing as the stress persists.

The stress buildup is the reaction, and the demand (or stressor) is the cause. The demand can actually be positive. Imagine your editor calling you up and telling you that she wants a new book from you. That's lovely — unless you can't see how on earth you can fit writing it into your schedule. It is lovely to be wanted, but her call still creates a demand — and stress.

Of course, the demands can be negative — bills coming due, pressure from your mate to make some money from your art, and on and on. Life is full of demands of these sorts, both positive and negative, and hence it is also full of stress.

In the psychological literature you will hear about "good stress" (called eustress) and "bad stress" (called distress). But it isn't the stress that is good or bad — it is the stressor. The stressor or demand may be positive, as in an editor wanting a book from us, but the stress produced nevertheless wears on our system. We may desire a certain stressor like a book deal, but the accompanying stress is still a problem. The cause may be a blessing, but the effect is a challenge.

Some demands are more objectively demanding, and some demands are more subjectively demanding. If I am hanging by my fingernails to a window ledge, I am in a physically demanding situation that would tax anyone. But what if, according to the terms of my contract with my publisher, I have ten months left to write my book? Do I need to construe that as a demand, a pressure, and a stressor, or can I normalize the situation and talk myself down from the stress I'm experiencing — say, by telling myself that ten months is an adequate amount of time to write the book (if, of course, I sit down and write each day)?

We can normalize or even reframe many demands as opportunities, and when we do, the associated stress vanishes. If you are holding it as lovely to make three calls today to gallery owners instead of as something dreadful that you wish you could avoid at all costs, you have changed the demand characteristic of the situation to one of opportunity. Only you can do this work of changing certain aspects of your life from demands to opportunities.

Let me repeat this point: you are stressed when something

feels demanding, and if you can make it feel enjoyable instead, it will not produce stress.

Even if we can't reframe or "think away" a stressful situation, we can still take action. Even when a demand remains demanding, you can reduce your stress level by engaging in smart stress-reduction activities such as progressive-relaxation techniques and deep-breathing techniques.

By the same token, many demands must simply *be met* if we are to reduce our stress. If our book manuscript is due in two months, we need to get it done in two months to eliminate that stressor. If we don't get it done, the stress will remain — with all sorts of new stress piled on top of it. Actually meeting demands reduces stress. If you are demanding of yourself that you contact fifty galleries, and if you find that demand completely reasonable, then the only way to reduce your stress is to begin to systematically approach those fifty galleries — even if approaching them makes you anxious!

This is an important point: *to reduce your stress you may have to increase your anxiety.* Take a moment to let that sink in.

It can also make great sense in some situations to substitute one set of demands for another and one set of stressors for another. Why? Because it may be that the old demands just couldn't be met, leaving you perpetually under stress, but the new demands can be met, lowering your stress levels. Here's an example.

Say you've demanded of yourself that you earn your living by painting, but the bills are piling up and you are under a lot of stress. It may be impossible to meet that demand right at the moment — that is, there may simply be no way to suddenly start earning your living by painting. So you may have to do the thing that likely will disappoint and sadden you — that is, try to find some reasonable day job so that the demands of the bills get met, while at the same time redoubling your efforts to make a living by painting.

The pressure of needing to make money from painting will no longer amount to the same demand, now that your survival needs are being met. In this scenario you've reduced your stress without abandoning your dream — just as long as you *don't* abandon your dream. This is an example of changing the demand structure of your life by opting for demands that can be met, like the demanding nature of a day job, rather than a demand that can't be met at this time, like earning your living by painting.

It's also vital to think through which of your stressors you yourself are creating. If you are demanding that you love the next paragraph you write, that demand — and that stressor — is entirely on your shoulders. Why not just show up and write and leave the appraising for later? By switching from attaching to outcomes to just showing up, you will reduce the nature and number of demands you are putting on yourself — and as a result you will lower your stress level. It is much less stressful to write a book than to write a book and need it to be great every inch of the way. Needing it to be great as you write it creates a huge amount of stress — stress that may even prevent you from writing.

Remember that stress builds up. Say that you find writing your novel very demanding. That means that day one hundred of writing your novel will not be the same as day fifty of writing your novel — by day one hundred it's likely that you are under more stress than you were earlier in the process. This should help explain why projects stress us out — they remain demanding until the very end, and as we continue to tackle them the stress keeps building up in our systems. Therefore, you will need to be even more mindful of using your stress-reduction techniques as your work progresses — because the stress is *building*.

Because these points are so important, let me summarize them here:

1. A stressor is any demand made on us by the outside world or by ourselves.
2. Some demands can be normalized or even reframed as opportunities.
3. Even if we can't get rid of a demand, we can still work to reduce our stress by using stress-management techniques.
4. If we can meet a given demand, we should do exactly that so that we can eliminate the stress. Sometimes trying to meet that demand will make us anxious, so we need to live with that reality. We may need to make ourselves anxious in order to reduce our stress.
5. We should think through whether it makes sense to substitute a new set of demands for our current set so that we can begin to deal with a demand that in fact can be met.
6. We must grow aware of the unnecessary and unhelpful demands that we put on ourselves — demands that increase our stress level and reduce our ability to perform.
7. Stress accumulates. Stress chemicals continue to build up in our systems if we don't do anything to lower them. Therefore, the deeper we get into a creative project, the more we need to engage in our stress-management techniques.

Varieties of Stressors

Let's name some of the major demands put on us either by life or by our own personalities. Here are eight stressors that most artists face:

1. Economic stress

- the stress of making a living
- the stress of providing for ourselves and for others

- the stress of making a living from something that we can't really tolerate doing
- the stress of dependency, if we are being supported by someone else

2. *Marketplace stress*

- the stress of trying to fathom what the marketplace wants
- the stress of trying to understand how the marketplace is changing
- the stress of hawking our wares and competing
- the stress of dealing with marketplace players

3. *Relationship stress*

- the stress that comes with *any* relationship, professional or personal
- the stress that comes when we aren't in a relationship and want to be in one (that is, the stress of loneliness and isolation)
- the stress of working out how to relate with our artist peers, with audience members, and with people whose opinions matter to us
- the stress of dealing with children, parents, siblings — that is, powerful everyday family stressors

4. *World stress*

- the stress produced by our economic and political realities
- the stress produced by the daily news
- the stress produced by natural disasters and the threat of natural disasters
- the stress produced by war, famine, and everything else the world delivers

5. Creative stress

- the stress produced by the realities of the creative process
- the stress produced by the difficulty of a given project
- the stress produced by coming up with good ideas
- the stress produced by trying to do good work

6. Existential stress

- the stress produced by our understanding that we have only a finite amount of time and that the clock is ticking
- the stress produced by having to make our own meaning (whether we want to or not)
- the stress produced by our creative efforts mattering so much
- the stress put on us by our doubts and fears that anything matters

7. Physical stress

- the stress produced by not getting enough good sleep
- the stress produced by working a lot of hours
- the stress produced by the physical nature of the work we do, say, if we're a dancer or an opera singer
- the stress produced by chronic illnesses, injuries, or disabilities

8. Psychological stress

- the stress produced by our personality shadows
- the stress produced by our simmering conflicts, say, between wanting to be an artist and needing to make money
- the stress produced by wanting to change and disappointing ourselves by our meager efforts at changing

- the stress produced by defensively walling off information that we don't care to look in the eye

We can't completely eliminate stress because we can't completely eliminate demands. Life is demanding, and we make demands on ourselves. But we can learn how to reduce a substantial portion of that stress. Here are some important strategies implied by our previous discussion.

Can you reframe the demand as an opportunity? Or can you simply ignore the demand? Many potential stressors are best ignored. With regard to any external stressor, start by asking yourself, "Can I make this go away simply by not focusing on it and by reorienting away from it?" Maybe something is happening in the world that matters to you but that you can't do anything about. You might decide that not focusing on it is better for your health than stewing about it. Can you reduce your stress by having this issue matter less to you? If the answer is yes, then you would do the cognitive work necessary to eliminate the stressor.

Is it possible to switch out the demand for some other demand that you may be able to meet more easily? If none of these options are available to you — if you can't ignore the demand, reframe the demand, switch it out for another demand, and so on — then your next step is to create an action plan, the best one you can devise at the moment, one that is as real as you can make it, and then to embark on it.

Your plan might include some or all of the following general stress-reduction techniques. It might include regular progressive relaxation. This is the very simple and useful practice of tensing individual muscle groups for several seconds and then releasing the tension, allowing muscles to gradually relax. For me, stress builds up in my neck, and I use a two-minute muscle-relaxation technique to quickly and effectively get rid of that stress.

Another technique is the Relaxation Response devised by

Dr. Herbert Benson. You sit comfortably, close your eyes, and relax your muscles. You focus on your breathing and continually repeat one word aloud or in your mind. It can be a word like *relax*, *easy*, or *om*. This technique is easy to learn and can make a big difference when stress starts building up. Or you might try guided visualizations. Get into a comfortable position, close your eyes, and visualize a scene that you associate with safety and relaxation. It doesn't matter what you visualize, just as long as it's calming to you. As you relax your mind, you also reduce your stress levels.

You might also try writing your stress away. Research reported in the *Journal of the American Medical Association* suggests that writing about stressful situations and experiences can reduce your stress levels — and lead to improvements in immune functioning, fewer visits to the doctor, and an increased sense of well-being. (The only thing you have to watch out for is that you don't start substituting writing about your stress for writing your novel!) And of course there is always exercise. Even just stretching and moving around can help reduce your stress levels, and a bike ride, jog, or yoga class can do wonders.

There are no perfect or complete answers because life keeps making its demands, many of which are difficult to meet. Nevertheless, you can use many strategies to at least lower your stress level. Let's look at a few of these as they relate to the stress of marketing your creative efforts.

The Stress of Marketing Art

Below I've listed several stressors that arise when you try to market your art, and made some suggestions for how to more effectively deal with those stressors.

1. *Thinking about selling your art*

   Strategy: Acquire an anxiety-management tool or two.
   Few people consciously practice anxiety management.

Every artist should. The techniques available to you include breathing exercises (one deep, cleansing breath can work wonders), brief meditations, guided visualizations (where, for example, you picture yourself relaxed and calm), discharge techniques (for example, releasing your pent-up anxiety through "silent screaming"), personality work (for instance, practicing acting as if you feel confident), cognitive restructuring (that is, changing the things you say to yourself and thereby reducing your experience of anxiety), and so on.

2. *Not knowing what to say*

Strategy: Practice what you intend to say. You should be able to say about your painting, "This is one of a series of paintings I'm doing that emphasizes the horizontal element in landscape." It doesn't matter if that is what you are really doing in your painting, since what you are really doing is beyond language. You are simply providing yourself with something better to do than grunt, mutter, ramble, and fumble. Second (and in seeming contradiction), do not feel that you need to have something "perfect" to say. Relax! But also be prepared.

3. *Dealing with people who hold the power and the purse strings*

Strategy: Do some inner work on feeling equal. Although it is not easy, it is possible to rethink the way you envision marketplace players, reminding yourself that your goal is to feel neither inferior nor superior to them but as if you and they are in the art-buying-and-selling enterprise together. If your tendency is to feel superior, remind yourself, "No smirking!" If your tendency is to feel inferior, remind yourself,

"Backbone, please!" Our typical reaction to power is a version of the fight-or-flight response: we want to strike first, or we want to run and hide. The less you hold these interactions as threatening, the less your fight-or-flight reflex will kick in and the more equal you'll be able to feel.

4. *Feeling pressured to "sell yourself"*

Strategy: First, begin to enjoy selling yourself. Since that is what you are obliged to do, you might as well enjoy it! Have nice things to say about yourself, couched beautifully so that you don't come off as too arrogant or grandiose. Drop well-crafted nuggets about your successes and accomplishments. Be your own best friend and advocate. Who else will be? Second, disidentify from each of your products. You are not your painting, and you do not have to die a little death if your painting is not wanted by some person. You can — and should — announce its merits and advocate for its value without, however, attaching to the need for a positive outcome. Say, "I really enjoyed painting these floating roses. I think they work very well!" Smile, and cherish having no expectations.

5. *Dealing with people who dismiss you*

Strategy: Be professional. Try not to burn bridges. Try not to act out. Try not to react much at all. If the person who dismisses you is cruel and insulting, protect yourself from that person but also decide whether it is worth it to respond and get embroiled in a drama. That drama could cost you sleepless nights and days missed in the studio. If the dismissal is just an everyday rejection, one of the countless we must face because we have chosen to create, merely shrug and persevere.

6. *Not feeling up to asking*

Strategy: Often we are unwilling to ask — for a gallery show, for space in a boutique shop, for the name and email address of somebody it would be good for us to contact, for a favor from a friend who knows somebody we ought to meet, and so on — out of anxiety or pride, or, in some cases, because we feel that we ought to be able to reciprocate in some way. As to the first, anxiety management is the key. As to the second, you need to talk yourself off your high horse by reminding yourself that you in fact do need lots of help in life. As to the third, if you feel that you have no way to reciprocate, remind yourself that you do not have to repay a favor the instant it is granted. Just say thank you and remember that you owe a good turn.

The Stress of Transition and the Stress of Checking In

A creative person encounters all sorts of stressful demands. Let's look at two now. The first is the stress of having to shift gears from our everyday mind to our creative mind, which, it turns out, is no easy matter.

All day long we are pressured to do things right and to get things right: to drive on the correct side of the road, to keep our checkbook balanced, to show up on time. Then a moment is supposed to arrive when we shift gears and allow ourselves genuine permission to make all the mistakes and messes we want in the service of our art.

Somehow we are supposed to fluidly move from the pressure of getting things right to the pressure of venturing into the unknown. Since it is not at all easy to make this transition, many creative and would-be creative people fail, on any given day, to move from the one state to the other.

How can you deal with this particular stress? One of the

best ways to help yourself create every day is to craft a starting ritual that you use routinely. When your ritual becomes habitual, you will find yourself moving effortlessly from your everyday life to creating.

You might, for instance, practice the following ritual. Make a cup of your favorite tea. In the minute or two it takes for the water to boil, take a few deep breaths, clear your mind, and ready yourself for work. Take your cup to your work space, and as the tea steeps prepare your materials. When your tea is as dark as you like it, put the tea bag on a small saucer and turn to your work.

Work until your tea is cool enough to drink. What is likely to happen is that you will lose yourself in the trance of working and discover that your tea is cold by the time you turn to it. Excellent! Part of your work ritual can be reheating your tea in the microwave as your first small break between creative stints.

Here are some other starting rituals. Do something physical like yoga, tai chi, or stretching. After five minutes of exercise, move directly to your creative work. Or meditate for five minutes. Once you've calmed your mind, mentally bring forth your creative project and hold it gently until you feel ready to proceed with it.

Or start each work session with a war cry. Stand up, beat your chest, and shout, "Ready! Set! Go!" Stride fiercely to your work space. Or choose a small object like a pebble or coin to serve as your talisman, and lovingly squeeze it several times before beginning to work. Craft your own starting ritual, or try out one of these.

Another special source of stress for those of us who do creative work with a deadline is the need to check in: with our editor, the gallery owner who is waiting for our paintings, or someone else with whom we don't really want to speak while we are lost in the wilderness of process. As much as we don't want to carry on that conversation, we must.

Consider the following scenario. You have four paintings due for a group show that is hanging early next year. You are supposed to provide the framed paintings by the first of the year. Things aren't going well, and the last thing you want to do is admit to the gallery owner that you've fallen behind. Unfortunately, you're meeting with him on Friday to talk about the show. What should you do?

For starters, here are seven things *not* to do:

1. *Don't take to your bed.* Hiding under the covers is not the answer. Even if you're feeling sad and overwhelmed, try not to throw in the towel. It can feel as warm, inviting, and safe in bed in these circumstances as it did back in childhood, but as an adult you're harming your career and battering your self-image if you avoid the situation.

2. *Don't cavalierly blow it off.* Don't adopt an attitude of "the hell with it!" and get it into your head that it doesn't matter, that you're too special to be held to rules, and that the gallery owner is a small-minded bourgeois for requiring deadlines. This attitude may make you feel good for a minute as you bask in your "I don't take anything from anybody!" glory — but then you'll remember all that you're losing.

3. *Don't make yourself sick.* There is no denying the mind/body connection and the fact that anxiety and stress make people vulnerable to illnesses. Ventilate your emotions and practice anxiety management so as to avoid getting sick. Learn some discharge technique such as silent screaming to ventilate pent-up stress, and adopt some anxiety-management techniques such as deep breathing and guided visualization to reduce your experience of anxiety.

4. *Don't go to the meeting and lie through your teeth.* Don't show up with a smile on your face and the intention to tell big, fat lies about your situation. To be sure, it behooves you to speak carefully and strategically about

what's going on and not to paint a bleak picture that causes the gallery owner to doubt you and file you in the "never again!" category. But there's a world of difference between speaking carefully and lying outright.

5. *Don't go to the meeting and act out or start apologizing.* Don't show up with the intention of thumbing your nose, asserting your independence, or making a scene — leave your arrogant persona at home. By the same token, don't show up and immediately start apologizing — leave your meek persona at home as well. These shadowy aspects of personality do not serve you and have no place at business meetings.

6. *Don't go to the meeting drunk or high.* If you regularly show up at important meetings and events drunk or high, get into recovery. If substance abuse or substance dependence is an issue for you, make recovery a top priority.

7. *Don't go to the meeting and start excusing yourself or blaming others.* You may have good reasons for falling off schedule, like the flare-up of a chronic illness, and legitimate gripes about the actions of others, like the disrupting influence of your teenage son's recent antics. But unless you are asking for an extension, the bottom line remains the bottom line, and the only real issue is whether or not you will get four strong paintings to the gallery owner by the first of the year. If that is still your intention, there is no payoff in complaining, excusing, or blaming.

What should you do instead?

1. *Get to work!* Not only will you make progress on your paintings and honor your commitment by getting right to work, but you will also put yourself in an entirely different frame of mind for the meeting

and change what you can legitimately report. You will feel better, and you will also be able to say with a straight face, "Boy, did I work well this week! It's been a joy getting to the studio!" If you hadn't started painting again, this would amount to a bald-faced lie. Since you did start painting, it is the absolute truth.

2. *Plan for the meeting.* Decide what outcomes you want. Do you need some clarification or some help from the gallery owner to get on with your work? This might sound like "I think we never quite got clear what size these four paintings should be, and I think that's been a bit of a stumbling block for me. Can we go over that?" Do you want to carefully test the waters to see if turning in two paintings rather than the promised four might fly? This might sound like "My crystal ball tells me that I'm going to have two excellent paintings ready by the first of the year, and I can't quite tell about the other two yet. How should we play that?" Prepare your agenda.

3. *Calculate how you want to present your situation.* Think through the precise language you want to use — your talking points. Have a response prepared for each of the questions you predict you might be asked. For instance, to the predictable "How's it going?" you might prepare the reply "Well, it's been quite a process! I've had my ups and downs, but this has been a good week." To the predictable "This is going to be some strong work, right? I'm looking for your best stuff!" you might prepare the reply "If this birthing process is any indication, these should be first-rate!" Think about what you might be asked, and prepare your answers.

4. *Show up as an equal, not a supplicant, in as cheerful and enthusiastic a mood as possible, with the intention of serving your interests, comporting yourself professionally, and conducting a little business.* If you're lucky,

you'll have to negotiate scores of meetings of this sort over the course of your art career. Even if you've fallen behind, and even if you're struggling to deal with your stress, try to put your best foot forward and make the most of these important interactions.

In a War-Torn Country

I was giving a weeklong workshop in Manhattan, and a writer emailed me to see if I had time for a session. We met in the West Village, on a bench in a quiet church garden. He arrived first — unusual, because I am always early.

"I take cabs," he said by way of explanation. "The subways scare me. Did you know that the Paris subways scared Dalí? He took cabs everywhere in Paris — even in the beginning, when he couldn't afford them."

I nodded. "*Scared* is an interesting word. What do you mean?"

"My nerves are raw," he replied. "For the past several years I lived in a war-torn country." He named the country. "That's my home — and it's never been safe there. It's been unsafe in the worst possible ways, in ways that make you hate our species. The things people have done to one another are unspeakable."

I took a guess. "And that's what you're intending to write about?"

He shook his head. "Yes and no. To write about them directly would be just too horrifying. To write about them indirectly is feeling too lenient — that way the truth will get lost. So I'm playing with ideas, images — I'm not there yet. I don't want to put all the inhumanity in there, but I'm not sure what does go in this novel."

He lit a cigarette and smoked it intensely.

"And your nerves aren't letting you get on with it?" I asked.

"Yes. I'm a wreck, a real wreck for a young man. I have boils on my neck, I can't sleep, I have stomach pains. I know

I should be doing things — learning Zen, getting massages, maybe taking anxiety medication — I don't know. My worst fear is that my constitution is not equal to this novel-writing process, which is incredibly taxing if you are trying to write something real."

I nodded. "And you're intent on writing?"

"Of course. There's nothing else for me. It's not just about witnessing what went on in my country. It's simply that there's nothing else for me. If I don't write novels I might as well jump in the Hudson right now."

"How do you live?" I asked.

"I wait tables at an expensive restaurant. I make enough money."

"That doesn't add to your stress?"

"No, not particularly."

We sat quietly. Manhattan seemed very far away. The sun shone brightly. Butterflies flitted among the flowers.

"One goal," I said, "is to remember what happened without reliving what happened."

He glanced at me. "Tell me more about that."

"You want to write about things that are making you physically sick to think about. It isn't just that you're getting sick. It's that you're also unable to find your fictional way. The experiences are too real to you and they, so to speak, demand to be photographed rather than fictionalized. I wonder if there is a way you can stop being there and start being here?"

He thought about that for a long time. "Right here in this garden, with you at this second, I know what you mean. I almost think that I could find the motif for my novel right at this second, because your presence...makes it safe. I know what you mean. In my body, I am always still in my country. I live in New York, but I am back there. The second I try to think, I have some kind of attack. Although, in this garden..."

"It feels right here?"

"It does."

"Then do some writing."

It took him a moment to understand what I meant. Then he pulled his laptop out of his backpack, booted it up, and lit a cigarette. He opened several files, moved them around, and got himself ready. Finally there was nothing to do but face it.

For five minutes he smoked and fidgeted. His mind hoped to arrive at the right motif for a novel; his body was living in a war-torn country.

"Be here," I said. "Try to be a writer, here in New York, working on a novel."

He reached for his pack of cigarettes, then changed his mind. He took a deep breath. He shut his eyes. He himself was the battleground. But finally the truce came. His fingers began moving over the keyboard.

He wrote for twenty minutes. I enjoyed the afternoon sun. Not a soul passed us that whole time. Just outside the walls of the garden, thousands of New Yorkers rushed to and fro.

Suddenly a car horn honked angrily. That broke the spell. He glanced up.

"Just stay quiet," I said. "A car honking is nothing. Keep it in perspective. It's not a threat, it's not important, it's nothing."

He nodded and returned to work. Soon dusk began to settle.

"We have to be done," I said. "It's time."

He nodded, took a deep breath, saved the file, and placed the computer beside him on the bench. Then he turned to me.

"What are my chances?" he asked.

I had to laugh. "Of what? That this novel will be easy to write? Zero. That rape and murder will stop? Zero. That you'll have a completely stress-free life? Zero. That you can do the work you intend to do and deal with your stress? You tell me."

"Nine percent," he said, smiling. "Wow. I am an incredible bundle of nerves. I have to do something. I have to — I have to repeat today's experience. I have to get this quiet and feel this safe. Without you around to protect the space."

"Yes."

"I want to be able to get this quiet and feel this safe."

"Yes."

"At least I have a picture of what I need. A new experience."

"Yes." I got up. "Stay and write. I have to go now."

He got up too. "Thank you."

As I left the garden I glanced back at him. He was still writing.

The Endlessly Demanding Nature of Life

Life is full of demands, and many extra demands are placed on artists. So our lives will be stressful. We can do many things to reduce our experience of stress, from reframing a given demand as an opportunity to ignoring a lot of those demands to getting some exercise. If you don't reduce your stress, it builds up, makes it harder for you to create, and makes you vulnerable to illness. It is essential that you factor stress management into your plan for leading your best life in the arts. Dealing with stress effectively should be one of your priorities.

You can begin by answering the following questions:

- What are your current stressors?
- What unhealthy strategies are you employing to deal with these stressors?
- What healthy strategies are you employing to deal with these stressors?
- What new stress-management strategies do you want to learn?
- What sort of stress-management program would you like to put into place?

Honor the reality of stress — and make plans for dealing with it.

Chapter 6

THE EMPATHY KEY

The word *empathy* refers to the (often-hard-to-achieve) realization that other people exist and have their own thoughts, feelings, and needs. It is the awareness of that reality, and it can also be the marriage of that awareness with some compassion in our dealings with those other real people.

You are creating for yourself, but you are also creating for other people; you are relating to other people; you are working with marketplace players and selling to your audience — all this requires that you understand the reality of other human beings and, to a certain extent and in a measured way, that you care about them.

A creative life requires that you remain aware of others and that you exhibit some fellow feeling. You do not want to give too much of yourself away in the process, but you *do* want to know what it feels like to walk a mile in someone else's shoes.

103

One unfortunate but typical way for artists to behave is to picture buyers as people who deserve to be manipulated and who must be reached by virtue of sales tactics that play on human weaknesses such as greed and envy. A second, better way to behave is to picture buyers as your fellow human beings who can be met without manipulation and trickery. If the question is "Which behavior garners the better results?," sadly enough the answer may be the first. However, if the question is "How do you want to lead your life?," the answer is surely by practicing the second approach — by practicing empathy and by championing the principle that people do not exist only to be manipulated.

What does the phrase *practicing empathy* mean? It means developing your personality sufficiently that you experience people as real human beings with needs, desires, and a point of view rather than as props in your personal play. If you are a parent, it means recognizing that it hurts your child if you do not honor your agreements, if you fail to pick him up when you say you will, and if you strike him because you are upset and he is handy to hit. If you are a teacher, it means providing feedback in a humane and careful way and not, just because you possess the power, in cruel and toxic ways. If you are a soldier, it means understanding that the people you are killing are human beings and not characters in a video game. It means investing in the reality of other human beings.

This way of being may not help you get what you want as often as leading from unbridled self-interest might. I know someone who tends to get his way in his business dealings because he talks nonstop and argues for his positions with such seamless ferocity that you have no chance to voice an objection or present your side of the story. As a result, he does very well. He gets without giving, has you do his work, increases his share and reduces yours, and nicely grows his business. If you complain, he has no idea what you're talking about and will produce a thousand reasons why you are wrong. He is defensive, combative, and argumentative. As I say, he does very nicely.

You do not have to be like this person.

The average person is relatively defenseless against the extraordinarily resolute manipulations of the business sociopath. But while we may have great trouble protecting ourselves against them or dealing sensibly with them, that doesn't mean we ought to *become* them. You want to practice empathy not because it is the best sales tactic but because it is the honorable way to relate to other human beings. It is the least cruel way, the least harmful way, the least bullying way. It is the way we make ourselves proud.

Nor does it preclude sales! It *does* reduce the number of tactics we can use as we go about the business of selling our wares, but we embrace that reality because we don't want to live as if *ethics* were a silly word used only by fools.

Say you've produced a new series of twelve paintings. What would it look like not to practice empathy? Telling everyone that there is only one painting left and that they must hurry, even though all twelve remain. Telling everyone that the prince of Prussia has purchased three and that the queen of Sheba is about to snatch up the rest. Calling up two collectors and telling each that the other is about to grab up *Number 3*, the best painting in the series. Knowing that the series is weak and touting it as great. Talking befuddled little old men and little old ladies into buying. Tripling the price and giving everyone a 50 percent discount. Explaining that your paintings with the violent imagery would make perfect Christmas gifts. Twisting the arm of your sister-in-law and guilt-tripping your friend from college into buying. And so on.

All these tactics are practiced in business. And they work. But they are not the only ways to deal with other human beings. You can be as energetic, powerful, and assertive as you like and still practice empathy. You can advocate for your new paintings with great gusto by telling everyone that they exist, by making phone calls and sending out emails spreading the news, by approaching everyone on your contact list, by asking your friend John if he will bring your paintings to the attention of gallery owner Sue (but not demanding that he do so), and by articulating their virtues and doing an excellent job of expressing their value.

You can sell with great enthusiasm while still minding the rights and realities of others. Yes, by operating this way you write off many standard sales tactics. But countless avenues requiring only your energy and your acumen remain open to you.

Empathy is a word from developmental psychology. If our parents were genuinely responsive to our needs, it is likely that we developed an ability to empathize with others. But many people had a poorer experience that resulted in lifelong relational difficulties.

However, even if they had that poorer experience in childhood, it is their job as adults to heal those wounds and make the conscious decision to treat the people around them decently. That is what we want in the world of art sales and in the broader world as well. We begin with ourselves by practicing empathy and by treating potential customers and marketplace players as we would like to be treated.

Empathy is the ability to understand another person's thoughts and feelings and the desire to do just that. It is both understanding *and* willingness. It is the mind-reading, feeling-reading ability built into us that many of us have trouble accessing or do not much want to access. It is in many ways an inconvenient ability, because it makes the people around us real — and how much more convenient it would be if they remained unreal!

Why is it important to empathize? It's important for all sorts of simple, straightforward reasons — but let's focus on its importance for the sake of your career in the arts. If you don't really get what marketplace players are thinking and feeling, you are much less likely to be able to deal with them or sell to them. The better you understand other people, the better your chances for success.

Let's take a simple example. You sell a book to an editor. The book comes out. You present her with an idea for a second book, and she declines. If you take her at face value and take no interest in what she is thinking and feeling or what is going on in her world, all you are left with is a no. If, instead, you empathize with her as a person and with her in her position as editor, you have created at the very least the chance to get some more information — information that may make all the difference with respect both to selling her this second book and to selling *anyone* this second book.

Empathizing here means understanding your editor's reality. This has two separate and different meanings: understanding her as a *person* and understanding her role in her publishing house. Is she, as a person, someone who makes snap decisions but who can then be invited to rethink her snap decision based on rational arguments? Is she, as an *editor*, someone who has to answer to a lot of people about her decisions and who therefore needs to be armed — by you — with lots of good ammunition to present to those other people? If you don't think about these things, then you won't be aware of how much ammunition you should present her with when you first propose a project or of how to help her change her mind after she's said no.

Remember that although the word *empathy* contains the idea of compassion, it is not exactly the same thing as sympathy or compassion. At its heart it is the ability to put yourself in another person's shoes and fathom what is going on in human interactions. Understanding where your editor is coming from is different from sympathizing with her plight as a harried editor who is daily bombarded by hundreds of emails and different from feeling compassion for her inability to get her own book written.

The proper antonym of empathy, as we're using it here, is not *unfeelingness* but *misunderstanding*. The proof that we are not empathizing with people is that we find ourselves not fully understanding where people are coming from or even completely misunderstanding. To take a simple example, if you send your editor an email and take personally the fact that she hasn't replied to you in twenty-four hours, you are not empathizing with her situation — that is, you are almost surely misunderstanding where she is coming from.

Especially if you have given her something that she actually has to think about, it should follow that she needs some time to think about it. It may be your experience that in the past she has replied instantly to your emails — but think through whether this email is like those other ones. If she has replied instantly to your chatty emails with chatty emails of her own but in this email you asked her what she thought about your idea for your next book, you are failing to empathize if you expect that sort of email to get an instant response as well.

Most artists are susceptible to lots of these misunderstandings for two primary reasons. The first is that they don't get sufficient opportunity to deal with marketplace players and so don't have a clear picture of who they are, how they operate, and what their universe looks like. The second is that because marketplace players matter so much to artists and make them so anxious, they can't think very clearly about who these people really are. Marketplace players are lionized, demonized, and fantasized about — but rarely thought clearly about.

To repeat: there are real, concrete reasons why artists fail to empathize with marketplace players, two being that they deal with them too infrequently and that when they do deal with them the interactions matter so much. It follows that because you typically have too few interactions with marketplace players, you want to create opportunities to meet these people and learn about them for the sake of learning about their reality.

It may therefore benefit you to attend a writers' conference where many agents and editors are in attendance, not just for the sake of pitching your work but also for the sake of seeing these strange creatures close-up and beginning to fathom what makes them tick. The obvious follow-up point is that if you do go where these strange creatures congregate, you don't want to hang back and let your anxiety and pride keep you from meeting them, chatting with them, and so on. When you get the chance to interact with marketplace players, don't let your fears or your ego get in the way of learning what makes them tick.

You want to normalize your relationship with marketplace players and envision them as human beings rather than as mythological creatures. You do this normalizing by *thinking more than reacting or feeling.* Sympathy and compassion have a large feeling component, but empathy is much more about thinking. When you think about a literary agent, what she needs from you, and what her job actually entails, you want to be thinking rather than feeling anxious, feeling upset with the marketplace, feeling predisappointed that she won't want what you're selling, or feeling anything else negative with respect to her. In order to empathize we need to step back, think more, and feel less.

Remember that two people can relate, even an artist and a marketplace player! Two people can share common interests, affinities, and easy rapport; they can appreciate each other. Relating is possible. It is easy enough, if we get too much criticism or silence from the marketplace, to get it into our heads that it will never be possible to relate to marketplace players. You want to avoid going to that dark place of imagining that you will never be able to relate to them and decide instead that your best bet is to keep an open mind, think rather than feel, and practice empathy.

Practicing Empathy and Preserving Art Relationships

Let's say that you've gotten better at empathizing than most artists do and that you've made some nice, solid — and valuable — connections in the marketplace. What's next? *Continuing* to practice empathy for the sake of preserving those relationships. Let's take a moment and consider how you might preserve those hard-won relationships: your relationship with the one editor who really loves your work, your relationship with the one reviewer who always has something good to say about your music.

Sometimes it is simply physical distance and a lack of regular contact that begins to wear relationships down; sometimes it is interpersonal difficulty; sometimes it is the demands of life, which seem to steal all our time and leave little time left for even family and friends, let alone our contacts in the marketplace. Let's focus on one aspect of this larger theme, on preserving your relationships with difficult marketplace players, with folks who are important to your art life but whose personalities and relational styles set you on edge.

Imagine that you have an ongoing relationship with a difficult gallery owner — let's call him Jim — who, for no reason you can identify, always tries to make you feel small in your interactions with him. You have no idea why he's being so passive-aggressive; you suspect that he is very different with his customers than he is with you; and you also suspect that he would deal at least marginally differently with you if your work sold better in his shop. Be that as it may, you value your exposure in his gallery — while also hating your interactions with him. How do you preserve a decent working relationship in these circumstances?

First, you want to look in the mirror and make sure that you aren't the main source or a significant part of the problem. Not infrequently we get into the habit of interacting from our shadowy side — from our insecurities, from the part of us that feels run down by or disappointed with our lack of success, from the part of us that "just isn't going to take it anymore" — and by acting that way we make life that much harder for ourselves. Many artists (like all human beings) alienate their peers and their supporters by interacting poorly with them. Be wiser and more careful than that.

Don't make matters worse by adopting a negative or confrontational attitude. If you need to say something important to Jim, be direct and clear, but try not to deliver your message in a spirit of criticism or from a hurt or angry place. Opt for some genuine fellow feeling and some good graces, along with some straight talking. Our first job — and the place where presumably we have the most control — is to make sure that we are not contributing to the problem. Do your part well.

Second, learn to temporize. When you and Jim interact, try not to react. Try to maintain a little calming distance between hearing from Jim and responding to Jim. If you get an email saying that he intends to hang only two of your paintings, even though he promised to hang four, and the email comes with a gratuitous critical dig ("Of course, if you sold better I'd hang all four, but as it is I think that even two might be a stretch"), do not instantly send a heated reply.

If you like, open a new, unaddressed email and write a nasty reply filled with every curse word you've ever heard — and then delete the email. Take a deep breath. Walk around the block three or four times. Think. Instead of impulsively reacting from a hurt or angry place, decide how you want to respond. You might want to bite the bullet, not react at all, and say something innocuous like "Two will be a great start! And when those two sell, I know you'll want to hang the other two." Think through to what extent calling Jim on his rudeness or his betrayal really serves you, and base your decision on reason and pragmatism, not on impulse and hurt feelings.

Third, keep in touch even if you don't feel like it. Do more than send an occasional check-in email to those people with

whom you want to maintain a real ongoing relationship —
even if you find them unpleasant. Set up a meeting for coffee,
even if that eats into a good part of a Saturday afternoon. If
they live far away, have a phone chat. Try to meet them face-
to-face at least every so often. As you think about where to
take your next vacation, consider going somewhere where you
are represented and visiting with your art contacts. Keep them
in mind, and keep in real touch with them.

It may feel hard to keep in touch with someone like Jim
with whom you don't much want to interact. But if you want
Jim to continue representing you, then it makes sense to
maintain real contact — and maybe even in a spirit of genuine
friendship. Get in his shoes and his mind, and consider what
he might want to hear from you. Has an article been done
on you? Let him know. Have you posted a video on YouTube
of one of your painting adventures? Let him know. Think up
reasons to be in touch — not to be a pest but to maintain useful contact.

Artists often have only a few advocates in the marketplace,
and they really need those advocates to support their efforts.
If everyone wanted our wares, we might be much more cava-
lier about losing a connection here or there. Since in reality
not everyone is clamoring for our creations, we need to maintain and preserve the connections we've successfully made so
far. Just as it makes good sense to carefully preserve your art,
it makes good sense to carefully preserve your art relationships too.

If you have the good fortune to possess many relationships in the arts, then you will want to practice empathy in
all of them. If you are lucky enough to be represented in a
number of galleries, if you acquire a substantial number of
collectors, and if you become known in the wider world, then
you have the job of maintaining those many important relationships, bringing some forward as circumstances dictate
and letting others temporarily recede, and learning strategies

that allow you to keep in touch with marketplace players and with your audience without pestering them to death.

Begin by identifying in your mind your most important contacts. These are the folks who matter the most to your art career: the collectors who buy often and/or who buy your largest and most expensive pieces, the owners of the galleries where you sell the most regularly, the one art writer who has taken an ongoing interest in you and done a substantial article on you.

There may be no more than a dozen people in this category, and you want to treat each of them as an individual, sending Mark and Mary, your two most loyal collectors, an email about your latest work before you announce it to anyone else, or letting Jill the art writer know that a show of yours will be in a church space in Italy and wondering if that might make for an interesting article. You want to keep these folks in your mind, and you want to contact them regularly, even when you have nothing particularly special to announce, to remind them that you are actively working and that you are thinking about them.

You might also think of visiting them personally, especially if you have never met them. If your biggest collector lives in Hawaii and you are trying to decide between a beach vacation in the Bahamas and a beach vacation in Hawaii, let the fact that collector Mark resides in Hawaii be the tipping point. Contact him to see if he would like to meet, and, if he says that he would, choose Hawaii over the Bahamas.

If your most important gallery is in Manhattan and you know that you'll be traveling to the Lake George region of upstate New York, see if you can pencil a visit to the city into your schedule. You do not need to see folks in person all that often if you are maintaining regular contact by other means (like email and phone), but seeing them every once in a while is both smart and personally rewarding.

It would be wise of you to manifest your confidence and

go a step further. You might jokingly wonder aloud to collector Mark in Hawaii (who, remember, is on your side, having purchased a number of your paintings) whether he might want to throw you a little party while you're visiting to introduce you to his collector friends. Similarly, you might ask Frank the gallery owner in New York if he'd like to invite some collectors to have drinks with you and him when you hit the city.

Use opportunities of this sort not only to renew acquaintance with this important person in your life but also to allow this person to extend your circle of acquaintances while you're in town. You may well discover that he or she is more than delighted to do so and that you rise in the estimation of these influential people with your willingness to promote yourself.

It is in your best interests to maintain contact with the large number of people who cross your path. The easiest way to do that is to maintain an email list and to send out periodic announcements, perhaps monthly. You might maintain one list of collectors, one list of gallery owners who don't show you yet but whom you want to approach again and again until they show you, one list of local and nearby folks who would be interested in knowing about your local shows and open studio times, and so on. The longer these lists grow, the better.

Nor do you have to strain to think of things to say to these folks: you can send a simple one-line email (which busy people appreciate) that says "latest work" and show one new painting in that email. You can mention a sale you've made or a show you'll be in months from now, send along a quote or a video that's moved you, or share a bit of personal news. You don't have to wait for big news before contacting them; contact them regularly so that you never leave their consciousness for very long.

Try to spend a little time every day maintaining contact with some of the many people out there who matter or who might potentially matter to your art career. This is a great way to practice empathy in a business context. Today you might contact Jim; tomorrow it might be Mary; the next day it might be someone you don't know but whom you want to know. The day after that it might be everyone on your list. If you can't manage to do this work every day, set aside some real time every few days or at least once a week to think through what contacts you want to make — and then actually make them.

Empathizing with Marketplace Players

Next let's look at some concrete tips for empathizing better with marketplace players. Let's consider a singer/songwriter, Jane, who is in the process of making her own CD — that is, she is paying for it out of her own pocket. Jane has hired a well-known and very busy freelance producer, Jack, to work with her.

This process of making a CD is almost always fraught with plenty of difficulties, because Jane has to get studio time scheduled far in advance, because she is tied to Jack's availability, and so on. But a lack of empathy will only make this hard thing even harder. Here are ten tips for empathizing with marketplace players, using Jane and Jack as our example:

1. *When you want someone to understand you, be clear.* For example, Jane could say to Jack, "Can we get together some time in mid-March and work on the album a little?," but that doesn't really communicate enough about her needs or his reality. It would be better if Jane said, "I can book studio time on March 7, March 8, or March 9 at the following hours. Does one of those times work for you? If none of them work, can you give me some times that might? But I hope that one of these times *does* work, because the studio is booked up and it's going to be really hard to find other dates. So if you could possibly make it on March 7, 8, or 9, that would be great!"

2. *When you want someone to understand you, be brief.* It is empathic to understand that people are not helped when they are bombarded by a ton of information. For example, Jane could write Jack a long email about all the reasons she is having trouble getting her last few songs written, or she could say, "Ten songs are done and the last two aren't. How do you think we should proceed?" Not only is the latter more helpful and more empathic, but stating herself that briefly and clearly will help clarify matters for Jane herself.

3. *When you want someone on your side, be affirmative.* For example, it is not empathic to think that people don't notice when they are being criticized or that they won't get defensive. Jane could say to Jack, "I don't think you are hearing me when I say that I need the drums to be less assertive," which is a criticism. On the other hand, she could say, "I'm loving our process together! I only wonder if I'm being clear enough about the drums. I'd love it if they could be a little less assertive. Do you think that would be okay?" You try out the honey approach until you are forced to turn to vinegar — you don't lead with vinegar.

4. *Make sure that you've been heard by checking in and by asking questions.* Often just checking in isn't enough — you need to make sure that you've been heard and understood. Jane might write to Jack and say, "Did you get the long email I sent you the other day?," or she might write and say the more effective, "In that email I sent you the other day, I fear that I might not have been clear on a couple of points, specifically on the timing of our next recording sessions and on the matter of your hourly rate going up in June. Were my thoughts on those two matters clear?"

5. *Don't let your nerves stop you from delivering your message.* Jane may have something very important that

she needs to get clear with Jack, but the thought of dealing with him might make her very anxious. It isn't going to pay her to let her nerves get the better of her since he *is* producing her album and at some point she really must deal with him. Her best bet is to recognize that dealing with him makes her anxious, accept that reality, make use of one of her anxiety-management strategies, bite the bullet, and deal with him. When people matter to us the way that the producer of our album matters to us, we mustn't let anxiety keep us from communicating with them.

6. *When warning bells go off, hold your tongue, at least long enough to gather your thoughts.* Let's say that Jack says to Jane in the middle of a conversation, "Oh, I think I'll be bringing my rate up to market rate in June." Jane would want to think about her reply rather than to blurt out, "But we agreed to work through the end of this album at your current rate!" or "I'm not going to be able to handle a higher rate — this is a disaster!" By holding her tongue and taking the time to gather her thoughts, she will do a better job not only of saying what serves her but also of intuiting where Jack is coming from — that is, a better job of empathizing with him. Having done that careful work, she can send Jack an email that is affirmative, brief, and clear that either asks for clarification about his passing remark or spells out her arguments for his continuing to work with her at his current rate.

7. *Never treat marketplace communications cavalierly.* If you are Jane and during a recording session you're disappointed with the way your bass player played, you don't want to say to Jack, "We need a new bass player!" — not if you are just beginning to think the matter through and haven't really decided whether or not you want a new bass player. If you bring it up

before you really mean to, you've made internal work for Jack, who now has to worry about the whole bass player question. Empathizing in this instance means realizing that when you bring something up, the other person is likely to begin thinking about it. If you don't want him to begin thinking about it yet, don't say it.

8. *Respond to marketplace messages in a calculated way.* Let's say that Jack mentions to Jane that he is getting married in June. Jane can congratulate him and think nothing more of it; or she can reckon that with a marriage comes a honeymoon and that he is going to be much less available in June than he otherwise might have been. That is simple empathy, to understand that a person who is getting married is likely to get busy, both externally and internally. So she can congratulate him *and* say the following thing that is calculated to help herself: "Wow, Jack! That probably means that May and June are going to be awfully busy for you, so I wonder if we could maybe book some extra hours in April to make sure that the project gets done?"

9. *Get brilliant about hidden agendas.* Let's say that Jack says to Jane about a song that he previously seemed to like, "This song about horses isn't quite there yet — I wonder if you want to take some time and get it ready before we go into the studio again?" If Jane takes this message at face value, it will probably sound like criticism and it may, in fact, affect her relationship with Jack and even make her doubt her song and her album. But if she is smart about human nature and the extent to which people carry hidden agendas, it may occur to her that perhaps something else is going on. So she might reply, "That's an idea — but I wonder if something is going on in your life and you need some time away from my project? Is that why you're wanting me to take another look at the horse song?"

She may have guessed right, or she may have guessed wrong; but by checking with Jack in this way, she has a shot at unearthing Jack's secret agendas, if there are any, while at the same time not getting down on the song or herself. Jack's comment may in fact have had nothing to do with her song, a fact that she won't learn unless she inquires.

10. *If you can't decode an important communication, ask for clarification.* Let's say that Jack says to Jane, "You know, I was working on Sarah's album yesterday, and I'm really falling in love with the way she holds her notes over the fade-outs." Jane may suspect that this message is intended for her, but unless she asks for clarification she won't actually know. If she doesn't ask she'll probably brood about whether or not Jack was trying to tell her something. Her best bet is to frankly ask, "Is what Sarah's doing applicable to my album, or were you just saying something nice about Sarah?" Whatever Jack's answer is, it is bound to clarify what, if anything, he intended by his remark.

Reading People

Martin came to see me because he "wanted to become a more creative entrepreneur." I asked him what he meant by this, since businesspeople tend not to mean the same thing when they use the word *creative* as writers or painters do. Sometimes they mean that they want to make more money; sometimes they mean that they need to think more innovatively in order to compete; sometimes they mean they have problems that need solving, having heard the phrase *creative problem-solving* bandied about.

Martin replied that he loved business but kept failing at it. His high-concept restaurant failed. His tech start-up failed. His consulting business failed. He claimed to have learned a lot from these failures, and he knew that the bios of successful businessmen were littered with such failures. But what he hadn't learned was why he kept failing. He wanted help thinking creatively about that.

"It sounds like you were able to raise money for these projects," I said.

"I was. They were good ideas, and other people thought so too."

"Then what would happen?"

"Well, the main thing was that I would always have partners who were impossible to work with. I've read every book there is on difficult people, but difficult people are way more difficult than the books let on. We'd get into power struggles, they wouldn't honor agreements, they had their own agendas — and the business would crash and burn."

"You knew this going in?"

He stared at me. "Knew what?"

"That these were difficult people and perhaps people to avoid?"

He thought about that. "No. I didn't know that. I must have terrible radar. I always think these guys are great!"

I nodded. "Why is that?"

"Why is what?"

"Why would you imagine that a fellow businessman was great, as opposed to just human? Especially after the second or third time of experiencing them in the real world?"

He thought about that.

"Human, how?" he finally said.

"Good and bad. Generous and selfish. Human."

"I don't think of people that way."

"You don't?"

He shook his head. "I give people the benefit of the doubt. I like to think that people are pretty much okay, if you treat them with respect."

"Your parents were okay?" I asked.

He shrugged. "We don't need to go there."

"We don't need to be real?"

"I just want some…creativity exercises," he said. "Maybe a way to brainstorm problems when they arise. Like creative communication skills. Maybe something along those lines."

"Uh-huh."

I let the silence lengthen.

"You can provide me with some of those?"

"No."

Martin stared at me. I could see him debating whether to stick with avoidance or accept the challenge.

"You're saying I'm naive," he finally said, frowning. "That I'm letting people walk all over me."

"*Naive* is an interesting word. What do you mean by it?"

He shook his head. "What I just said. Letting people walk all over me."

"If that's how you mean it, then I don't think you're naive. Because once you see that someone is walking all over you, you do something. You don't just take it. So let's find another word."

"Like what?"

"You tell me."

He gave that some thought. "It isn't a word. It's that I don't read people well. That still feels like *naive*."

We sat in silence.

"You have a new business idea?" I asked.

He nodded.

"And a prospective partner?"

"Yes."

"Tell me about him or her."

"He's great!" Martin exclaimed. "He —" He stopped.

"Exactly," I said.

"What do I mean when I say 'he's great'?" Martin said speculatively, speaking to himself. "What is it that I'm doing?" He sat pondering. "I think…this is funny. I think I have the idea that to know what another person is thinking is an invasion of his privacy. We had so many rules about that growing up! My parents needed their privacy. We kids had precious little. I think I've equated knowing what you're thinking with invading your privacy."

I nodded. "That realization is so smart. Now — what would you like to do?"

"What can you do?" he exclaimed. "How do you know what a person is thinking?"

"You can't, really."

"So? Then where are we?"

"Let's say I'm your prospective business partner. I say everything you want to hear, so you think I'm great. You can't read my mind — so how can you know who I really am?"

"That's the question!"

"That is the question. But you've never tried to answer it. You agree that the question matters?"

"Yes!"

"Then you must answer it."

He thought for a long time.

"It has to do with getting the baseline right," he said. "My baseline is off. Right now when I meet one of these guys, someone who's good at presenting himself, glib, confident, fast-talking, who has an answer for everything, I give his style a kind of mental check mark. Rather than saying, 'Wow, he is very glib,' I say, 'Wow, he is great.' I ignore the warning signs — I even take them as pluses! My baseline is off."

"Is there a simple way to articulate your new baseline?"

He stroked his chin. "It's…maybe it's…people are people."

"Excellent!"

"That doesn't mean that they're automatically jerks."

"No."

"But it does mean they're not automatically great."

"Exactly."

"And they have to be…watched."

"Yes."

"And read. I need to read people better. And I need to read them faster! And watch them when we interact."

"Because creative work like building a business requires it. You don't build a business only with bricks and mortar or ideas — you need people."

He nodded. Then he smiled. "So you weren't going to give me some brainstorming exercises? Or give me something 'creative' to do? You weren't buying my presentation?"

"Nope."

"Well, thank you."

I've had this same conversation with orchestra musicians, with documentary filmmakers, with scientific researchers, with dancers, with countless creative people who had never thought to include reading people among the skills they needed to cultivate. As if empathy were a luxury! Martin thanked me again and left deep in thought.

Empathy and Self-Consciousness

Sometimes we can't practice empathy because we are too anxious and self-conscious to be really present. If this rings true for you, it will pay you to try to reduce that self-consciousness. To learn this skill, you might begin to write conspicuously in public places, to find or create more opportunities to be your artist self out in the world, and, if you are a painter and even if it isn't your style, to paint en plein air. Here are some tips for doing just that: for venturing out, setting up your easel, and painting outdoors. If you work in a different art discipline, you'll need to think through how these tips might apply to you.

1. *Deal with your self-consciousness.* Most people don't enjoy looking and feeling conspicuous. Even exhibitionists prefer blending in most of the time! So you need to talk yourself into a willingness to be seen,

watched, pointed at, gawked at, criticized, and all the rest. You may turn out to be much more invisible than you fear you will be — but if you aren't, if people gather and watch you and gawk, so be it!

2. *Get ready for an infinite amount of visual data.* When you're in front of your canvas, you have only whiteness to look at, which can be its own problem. But that's a very different problem from the staggering amount of visual material available to you as you wander through the world and see forests or forests of buildings. Wherever you turn your head, there is more to see! Accept this reality and talk yourself into the belief that all this visual data is a special kind of abundance, not some sort of problem.

3. *Be prepared to choose.* You can't paint everything you see! Even if you could, what would be the point? Isn't the artistry in the choosing? Choosing provokes anxiety, and having to make strong, clear choices about what to paint may well raise your anxiety level. Be prepared for this anxiety, know what you're going to do to combat it, and accept that you have no choice as an artist but to choose.

4. *Create your kit.* You need a painting setup that works for you. This may take repeated tries, since the first setup may be too cumbersome, the second too meager, and so on. Learning how to feel comfortable en plein air is a process, and there is no reason why you should nail your setup the very first time. Consider your first tries experiments, and learn from them.

5. *Be clear about your intentions.* Are you planning to make finished paintings while you're out? Or loose sketches? Or something in between, something that's more than a sketch but that still requires work back at the studio? Maybe you don't know your intentions — in which case, try to learn them as you go. Maybe

you'll discover that you can complete things on the spot, and maybe you'll learn that your real goal is to capture a sense of place and finish up at the studio. Learn as you go.

6. *Think about partnering.* Would you enjoy going out with a friend? Maybe several of you could travel together? You don't have to confine yourself to one way or the other — usually Van Gogh went out alone, but sometimes he went out with Gauguin. Think through the pros and cons of painting en plein air with a buddy, and if the pros tip the scale in their favor, find a painting partner.

7. *Schedule real time.* Most people are so busy nowadays that they can't find three or four hours unless they consciously pencil those hours into their schedules. Look at your schedule and make some decisions about where you might find your en plein air painting time. If you can't find the time, that means that in order to get en plein air painting on your schedule, you will need to rethink how you spend your time.

8. *Focus on the joys and benefits.* Remind yourself of the potential joys of en plein air painting. You may be focusing on the difficulties associated with it, and by focusing on those difficulties you may have forgotten how joyful it is to be out in the world looking, seeing, and creating. Think back to how much you've enjoyed sketching in parks and cafés. The studio is great — but so is the world!

9. *Keep it simple.* Do not overdramatize the process. It isn't as if you're going to the ends of the earth! We can easily convince ourselves that something is far more difficult than it really is. Have a quiet conversation with yourself about how easy it will prove to gather up a few things, go out, and find some fascinating vistas to paint. Don't exaggerate the difficulties!

10. *Remember its importance.* Have a conversation with yourself about the importance of en plein air painting — and learning to be conspicuous — to your creative life. Honor your understanding of its importance, and make sure that you get some en plein air painting on your schedule — and soon!

Remember the central point here: that you want to do an excellent job at empathizing with people, that your self-consciousness can easily get in the way of your desire and your ability to practice empathy, and that en plein air painting is one way to learn how to deal with your self-consciousness. However, there are countless other ways. If you are not interested in en plein air painting, or if you are not a visual artist, then figure out your own way to become conspicuous, create your own tip list, and then endeavor to reduce your experience of self-consciousness through actual practice.

Simple Empathy

Empathy is not the callous reading of people for personal gain — the kind of empathy that psychopaths possess — nor an indiscriminate giving away of ourselves because we are "feeling so much" in our interactions with others. It is not a cold skill or gushy relating. It is simply our ability and our willingness to understand what is going on with other people.

To learn more about your ability to empathize, answer the following questions:

- What difficulties have you experienced by not understanding where another person was coming from?
- What *in you* prevents you from empathizing with others?
- What do you see as the best ways of dealing with difficult people?

- What kinds of relationships do you want to maintain with the people important to your creative life?
- How will you get better at empathizing?

It is very easy to get lost in our heads and to stay there and not have a very good idea of what other people, including marketplace players, are thinking and feeling. It may be that we think we can go it alone, but in fact every artist needs an audience, marketplace advocates, and other actual human beings who have their own thoughts, feelings, needs, and wants. When you get better at empathizing, you also get better at collaborating and at forging the relationships that serve you.

Chapter 7

THE RELATIONSHIP KEY

Relationships in the arts are complicated. You may be very friendly with a fellow painter and also quite envious of her. You may actively dislike a gallery owner or a collector but decide that he is too valuable to cast aside, maybe because he is your only advocate or your only customer. You may respect your editor's opinions but despise the rudeness with which she delivers them. There may be no such thing as a genuinely straightforward relationship anywhere in life, but relationships in the arts are that much *more* complicated and shadowy.

Let's try to tease out fifteen sensible rules for marketplace relating:

1. *You can't succeed in the marketplace without the help of others.* You can do whatever you like in your mind and you can do whatever you like in the studio, but if you want an audience, then you need help in the

marketplace. Even if you engage in the equivalent of self-publishing, you still need audience members if you want to feel successful. So, the first rule is that you can create as if you were on an island, but as soon as you want to share your creative efforts with others, you are embroiled in the world of others. There is just no getting around that.

2. *Your side of the relationship equation is up to you.* You get to decide how you want to be in your relationships, even if you feel pressured to be someone else. You get to decide if you want to be honest and straightforward even if others aren't, if you want to be polite and diplomatic even if others aren't, if you want to be quiet and calm even if others are stirring the pot and making dramas. It may not prove easy to be the person you want to be at all times and in all situations, since the marketplace has a way of throwing us off our game, but you can nevertheless hold the intention of trying your darnedest to be the "you" you would most like to be.

3. *Upgrade your personality.* You can't be the "you" you want to be in relationships if you're an addict, if you're running too scared, if your unhealthy narcissism has outstripped your healthy narcissism, if you approach life too defensively. We've been chatting throughout this book about the need to create a powerful, upgraded "you" that is equal to the challenges of a life in the arts. This is especially true as you begin to deal with the high-pressure dynamics of interviews, appearances, editorial meetings, and the other features of relating in the marketplace. Try not to make those already-tense interactions tenser by showing up as a weaker version of yourself.

4. *You do not have to be real in all your professional dealings with others.* You can make calculated decisions

that in your marketplace relating you will act friendlier than you actually feel, put on a more optimistic, positive face than the one you wear at home, not let people know about your secret reservations about your work or your secret doubts about their expertise — in short, you can and should create a persona that serves you.

5. *Know your intentions, and choose them wisely.* Do you want to ensure that your editor knows she's made a silly mistake, so as to get even with her for all the times that she's pointed out *your* mistakes, or do you want to keep working with this editor? Do you want to blow up your relationship with your gallery owner because you're embarrassed to tell him that you don't have paintings ready for your show, or do you want to do the smart thing, which might be to buy yourself more time and turn the negative into a positive by gushing about how wonderful your paintings will be, albeit a little late? If you come from your shadowy place, from a defensive place, from an unaware place, you're likely to ruin marketplace relationships that may be fragile to begin with. Be aware, and try to arrive at some smart decisions about your intentions.

6. *Expect people to come with shadows.* Everybody you deal with is a human being who comes with all the baggage that human beings come with, including hidden agendas, thin skins, passive-aggressive tendencies, self-interestedness, and so on. These everyday shadows do not disqualify them — if they did, no one would be able to deal with anyone. People come with light and shadows. Try to enjoy the light even as you stay aware of the shadows. If a person proves too shadowy and difficult, that's one thing, but if she remains in the wide middle range that most people occupy, just

learn to deal with her troublesome but ordinary shadowiness.

7. *Be strong when you need to be strong.* It may be smart and strategic to be pleasant, easygoing, and low maintenance in most of your marketplace interactions. But you also need to be strong when strength is required. If a certain moment calls for assertiveness, find that iron inside you. If your publisher wants to change the title of your book at the last minute to a title you just can't tolerate, speak up. You may have no real say in the matter, and all you can do if they won't budge is to cancel the contract, but by standing up and speaking your mind there's a decent chance you can positively influence the outcome. You may have to shift from genial and agreeable to hard-nosed in a split second. Get mentally ready for such eventualities.

8. *Make conscious decisions about who should get more of your time and who should get less.* That is, be strategic about the importance of people in your networks and your universe. If somebody is pestering you with question after question for a print interview and you find yourself spending more time responding to those questions than chatting with your editor about the revisions she's suggested to your novel, you are letting a squeaky wheel derail you. Decide on how you want to relate to people not on the basis of their aggressive demands but rather on the basis of what strategically serves you.

9. *Ask questions.* Marketplace players have plenty of reasons for not always being clear. They may offer you a publishing contract but prefer that you not know that their small press is on its last legs and that your book might never be published. Therefore, they leave out of the conversation any mention of your book's publication date. If you notice this omission, your

choices are to act like the omission must have been an oversight and nothing to worry about or to judge the omission a red flag and ask, "When will the book be published?" If you take the first route, you may be setting yourself up for big trouble, trouble such as the publishing house holding your book for a year or two and then announcing that it can't publish it. If, on the other hand, you ask, you may not be happy with the answer, but you will be in a better position to decide whether or not to proceed with this publisher. Ask questions, even if you feel one-down, even if you feel embarrassed to ask, even if you're not sure that the question really needs asking. Err on the side of clarity.

10. *Ask for help.* If you're having trouble figuring out how to reach someone you think would prove a wonderful endorser of your book, ask your editor to help. If you want to make contact with a journalist but you think that the contact ought to be made by your gallery, ask your gallery owner to reach out to the journalist. If you want to perform with someone and you have a friend who knows that someone, ask your friend to introduce you. If a deadline is approaching on a residency application and one of your referrers hasn't gotten around to writing a letter of recommendation yet, ask the person directly for the help you need, namely, a timely recommendation. Ask for help, and ask for what you need.

11. *Negotiate.* It is part of our repertoire of relationship skills to negotiate, but we tend not to use that skill with marketplace players because they intimidate us and because we fear that if we ask for anything, the deal will vanish. But if you're polite, careful in how much you ask for, and not attached to the outcome, you will discover that in virtually every case you will get more than you were first offered. You might get

a few thousand dollars more on your book contract, a slightly better cut on your split with your gallery owner, more advertising for your concert, or even just more time, say, by negotiating the delivery date of your book or the recording date of your album. Get used to negotiating: politely, carefully, and matter-of-factly.

12. *Do not give yourself away.* If someone you know in an arts organization asks you to volunteer your time and energy in support of something they are doing, think twice before agreeing. Of course it is great to be of service, and being of service is one of our prime meaning-making opportunities. But it is one thing to serve by supplying a guest blog post in support of an event and another to serve by spending a full year organizing a conference. Be very clear about what the commitment would amount to, check to see if you are tempted to agree just because so little else of interest is going on in your life, and make sure that you don't cavalierly give away your time and your energy.

13. *Try to make your personal relationships support your art intentions.* Let everybody in your house know that you are an artist, in case somehow they didn't pick up on that already, and that you need a certain amount of time and space in which to work and a certain amount of unconditional support from them. If they're old enough to take care of themselves in the morning, let them know, for example, that for those first two hours of the day they can make their own waffles and pick out their own clothes. Smile as you say these things — but get them said.

14. *Prepare simple answers to difficult questions.* It is much easier to relate, both to friends and family members and to marketplace players, if you've prepared answers to the common questions you'll be asked, such as "What are you writing?" or "Why are your paintings

so violent?" or "Why can't I hear your music on the radio?" Say, for example, that you're an independent filmmaker. What are you naturally going to be asked? "What's your film about?" "Who's in it?" "When will it be coming out?" "Did you have to use your own money to make it?" "How did your last film do?" "Can I get any of your films on Netflix?" And so on. These are obvious questions and, whether their intent is benign or malicious, they really should not surprise you. Just prepare simple answers and use them.

15. *Do not unnecessarily burn bridges.* If an editor rejects a manuscript, thank her politely and keep her in mind for the future. She is already one of those important people in your life, a marketplace player who actually bothered to read something of yours, and it is not at all outside the realm of possibility that she will buy something from you down the road. Even if you have to sever a relationship, try not to burn it to the ground. You may well be seeing that face again!

You want to protect yourself in your relationships, but you also want to be open to relationships, because without them you can't have the life in the arts that you want. You want to learn how to forge relationships, maintain relationships, and, when necessary, get out of them with as little drama as possible.

The Art of Self-Relationship

Nothing matters more than the way we relate to *ourselves*. In this section I'd like to provide you with a technique for entering into better self-relationship. The goodness of your other relationships — with loved ones, with marketplace players, with members of your audience, with everyone — flows from the goodness of the relationship you establish and maintain with yourself. That relationship is primary. So I want to teach you a method for keeping track of and improving your self-relationship.

It's a journaling technique I call the Focused Journal Method. You can use this technique as your regular and best way to analyze any issue, from understanding why a creative project is stalled to deciding how you want to relate to your editor to solving a personal problem.

Let me run down the steps of the Focused Journal Method before examining them in some detail:

Step 1. You identify an issue.
Step 2. You examine its significance.
Step 3. You identify core questions.
Step 4. You tease out intentions.
Step 5. You notice what shadows get activated.
Step 6. You identify the strengths you bring.
Step 7. You align your thoughts with your intentions.
Step 8. You align your behaviors with your intentions.

Most people rarely follow these steps, as straightforward, sensible, and effective as they are in helping us take strong action. Just ask yourself: When was the last time you really examined an issue in a focused way and got all the way from naming the issue to understanding the concrete thoughts and actions that would support its solution? It's probably been a long time, if ever.

Let's go through these steps now one by one.

The first step in this journaling process is identifying an issue to work on. This sounds easy in theory — maybe you want to lose weight, build your business, create more regularly, do a better job of dealing with your distraction addictions (Facebooking, watching reruns of *Desperate Housewives*, and so on). But everyone has *many issues* they want to deal with, and identifying *one issue* to focus on leaves all those other issues in the lurch. What to do?

As with other matters we've chatted about, the key here is to choose one pressing issue and commit to working on it. If you like, you can begin by generating as long a list of these important issues as you need to — and then see if these issues can be clustered and refined into a smaller number, say three or four. Those three or four issues might become *the* issues you focus on as you journal. Maybe your list will look like this: finish writing my novel, lose twenty pounds, take more risks, and make some connections in the publishing world.

Clearly these aren't *all* the issues in your life — but they are *plenty* to focus on. From those four you would choose one at a time to journal about, since it's very hard to focus on more than one thing at a time. However you arrive at the issue you want to work on, you must arrive there. Until you do, you haven't really started.

The second step is to examine the real significance of the issues you've chosen. Our minds can easily play tricks on us and cause us to believe that certain issues are significant to us even when they aren't. Maybe we've identified as issues that we want to lose "that last ten pounds," that we want to find a decent-paying part-time job, and that we want to make more time for friends. Are these really significant concerns to us, or are we merely repeating things we've been saying to ourselves for years?

There is no way to determine the true significance of an issue except by thinking about it, turning it around, and looking at it with fresh eyes. One way to go about this is to ask, "Do I mean it?" This sounds like "I say I want to lose those last ten pounds. Do I mean it?" If you come back with a resounding "Yes!" then you can feel reasonably confident that you do mean it. If you come back with a "No, not really," or "I'm not really sure," you have some more thinking to do.

If you're not really sure, the next logical question is "Well, then, why do I keep pestering myself about this issue? What's *really* going on?" You may discover that you don't want to lose those last ten pounds because you fear that when you do lose them you'll feel secure enough to leave your husband, an outcome you aren't ready to contemplate. It takes courage to ask, "What's *really* going on?" because you may end up with some disconcerting self-knowledge. All self-inquiry has this aspect of danger to it. So step two, examining the real significance of our issues, is really a call to courage.

The third step is to identify core questions associated with the issue you've identified. Let's say that you're a painter having trouble making sense of the next steps of your career. You decide that the issue you want to work on is marketing yourself more effectively. Your journaling process might sound like the following:

"Okay, I know that I need to market myself. This isn't a 'should' from somebody else's agenda but something that matters to me and that I have to own as important. So, what exactly am I supposed to do? There's so much advice out there — and so few painters making it! But I know that successful painters do exist, so let me try to stay positive…

"I think the central question I need to address is, 'Am I imagining that I'm going the gallery route, or am I taking some other route?' If I go the gallery route, what is the smartest way to proceed? If I mean to take some other route, what are those routes? I can create a website — but will that amount to anything but a very pretty business card seen by no one? If I don't get *publicity* and if I don't make a *name* for myself, what good is a pretty website? And won't galleries need an unknown like me to come to them with a name already — that crazy chicken-and-egg problem? So, doesn't it make sense to focus on 'getting a name'? But what does *that* mean?"

A journal entry of this sort represents a painter's honorable attempts at getting some core questions asked. She hasn't answered them yet — but the very act of naming them helps her gain clarity and points the way toward solutions. Once you've named your issues and articulated why they're important to you, then you begin to tease out core questions that will help you meet the challenges you've identified.

The fourth step is to tease out intentions. Let yourself move from thinking about things, journaling about things, and wishing things would happen to intending something and making it happen. Not only should journaling help you clarify what is going on, but it should also help you tease out clear intentions that sound like "I intend to finish my novel by April 1," "I intend to leave Harry before any more Thanksgivings arrive," or "I intend to manifest my self-confidence every day."

Until we arrive at clear intentions, we haven't really mobilized our resources or committed to a course of action. There's a world of difference between internally saying, "It would be great to get the garage organized" and "I intend to spend all day today getting the garage organized." The first has a nice enthusiastic ring to it but no real teeth. The second sounds like sleeves being rolled up and work commencing.

You identify an issue or issues you want to focus on, you double-check to make sure you understand the real significance of those issues, and you ask yourself some smart questions to help you clarify your intentions. Then you announce those intentions loud and clear.

The fifth step is to notice what shadows get activated as soon as you announce an intention. Every time we create a strong intention — to build our home business, to finish writing our novel, to speak up in our family, to take bigger risks at work — we activate our defenses and the shadowy parts of our personality. We instantly start to talk ourselves out of our intention by saying things like "I'm too tired" or "I'm too busy" or "Next week would be better." Such things regularly happen the instant we set a strong intention.

When you identify an issue that you want to work on and

tease out an intention, notice what shadows appear. For each shadow you identify, talk yourself through how you want to handle it. For instance: "Okay, the thought of talking to John about turning the spare bedroom into a painting studio makes me really anxious. So I am going to learn (and really practice!) one good anxiety-management strategy this week — and then have that scary conversation."

All your good plans are likely to come with some personality shadows. Expect those shadows, and learn to deal with them. If you ignore them, you'll find your plans repeatedly derailed.

The sixth step is to identify what strengths you bring to the table. We've gotten into the habit over the past hundred years, coinciding with the birth of psychotherapy, of being very aware of our flaws and our weaknesses. With our self-talk we regularly put ourselves down, and we are very good at internally announcing how we aren't equal to life's challenges. This dynamic goes a long way toward preventing us from recognizing the undeniable strengths we also possess.

If we don't actively identify and announce those strengths, we may forget we possess them. As part of your focused journaling process, after you identify an intention, also identify the strengths you can employ in realizing your intention. These might include your sense of humor (which you will need as you explore the gallery world), your skepticism (which will serve you in good stead as you peruse gallery contracts), your resilience (which you'll need in order to deal with inevitable rejections), and so on.

The seventh step is to align your thoughts with your intentions. If your intention is to lose ten pounds and all day long you think, "This is too hard!" and "I am so hungry!" and "What's that delicious smell?," you're unlikely to be able to stick to your eating plan. Once you've formed an intention like "I intend to lose ten pounds," you will want to remind yourself that in order to stick to your eating plan, you will need to get a grip on your mind and think thoughts that align with your intention.

Not only do you want to stop thoughts like "This is too hard!" and "I am so hungry!" but you also want to introduce thoughts that positively serve you, such as "I am happy with my new eating plan" and "I am looking forward to my late-afternoon treat." You create thoughts of this sort, and then you consciously think them throughout the day. Creating useful thoughts to think and then not thinking them doesn't really serve you! A great Focused Journal Method exercise is to create some thoughts that align with your intention and then to indicate when *exactly* you will think them (for example, first thing in the morning, whenever you start to feel a little hungry, and so on).

The eighth step is to align your behaviors with your intentions. Every intention implies a set of behaviors. If it's our intention to find a literary agent for our novel, that implies that we have written our novel, written a synopsis of our novel, located agents, and drafted a query email. These are the logical and necessary actions that connect to an intention of this sort.

Why don't we behave in these straightforward ways if they are the logical and necessary behaviors we need to manifest? For countless reasons: that it scares us to think about communicating with agents, that it bores us to write a synopsis of our novel, that it daunts us to figure out which agents to approach. We don't behave in these obvious and reasonable ways for all sorts of human-sized reasons.

By using your journal to identify what behaviors flow from your intentions, you make it very clear to yourself how you ought to be behaving. You may still have great difficulties following through, but just the act of naming those right behaviors and seeing them in print in front of you will bring you that much closer to realizing your intentions.

If you simply want to get down your thoughts and feelings

in a journal, no method is required. If, however, you want to engage in some real, systematic self-inquiry in which you tease out issues and come to conclusions about how you want to think and act, then a method like the Focused Journal Method can prove invaluable.

Next let's take a look at two faces of self-relationship.

The Buddhist Printmaker

A printmaker, who was also a practicing Buddhist, came to see me. He produced beautiful prints of traditional motifs like cascading waterfalls, scrub trees clinging to cliffs, and birds soaring in the mist. They sold brilliantly. But they gave him no joy. He didn't even know why he created them.

"I must not be very advanced," he said, shaking his head. "I still feel a need to have things matter. I know I should get over that!"

I had to smile a little. "Maybe you should give your prints away. That would be quite advanced. I have wall space for several of them."

He didn't laugh. He stared at me, thinking.

"The subject matter isn't the problem?" he asked after a while. "It's commerce that's the problem? The selling? If I made prints and I didn't need to sell them, do you think they would matter more?"

I shrugged. "What do you think?"

He thought about that. "No," he finally replied. "If I were producing work that mattered to me, I wouldn't mind selling it."

"All right!" I continued. "So commerce isn't the problem. For many visual artists the core problem is that with so much arresting natural imagery all around, why compete with it? Why make more images if there are things to see already, everywhere. Might that be it?"

Again he reflected. I could see him turning the question over. It is rare for people to actually bother to think — usually they respond with habitual, reflexive responses — and it is a very good sign when they do think. How else will solutions come?

"No," he replied. "I understand what you're saying. It's a valid point, an important point. You can't improve on nature, and nothing is really more arresting than what you can see while walking along a country lane or the street of any city. But a visual artist — a good visual artist —" He hesitated. "A great visual artist does something else. He does a one-in-a-million kind of thing — but I don't know how to say what that is."

I nodded. "But at least you know what you mean. So...tell me what you really want. Do you want not to want? Or do you want to do the great work you just alluded to?"

Again he thought for a long time. "Not so long ago I saw a retrospective of the drawings of George Grosz," he said. "I was completely transfixed. There's one watercolor called *A Married Couple*. For me, something about the whole Nazi era is captured in that watercolor. How can that be? How can you paint a watercolor of an ordinary couple and communicate so much about a hideous regime and a world war? Grosz could and did. I stand in front of that watercolor and marvel." He stared at me. "I want to do work like that."

"So you want to want?"

"I do."

"Create a sentence that makes some sense of your desire to want and your philosophy of detachment."

He pondered that. Slowly he nodded. "I get that. I need to really try — and if a certain image fails, so what? I go on to the next one. Really try — and then let go. 'Really try and then let go.' That works!"

"Okay! Now, about your waterfalls and mountains and trees —"

"They're beautiful," he interrupted. "But they're not important to me. They're beautiful but not important."

"What imagery would be important?"

"I don't know."

"That's the question, isn't it?"

"That's the question."

"So let's get that answered."

He laughed. "You don't go very slowly, do you?"

"No."

He closed his eyes and murmured, "What is my imagery?" He sat that way for a long time. I could see him picturing and rejecting imagery. Every once in a while he would shake his head, rejecting an image with particular certainty. Then something dawned on him. He turned it over several times in his mind's eye. He nodded and opened his eyes.

"I have it," he said. "I don't want to describe it, but I have it."

"Can you give it a shorthand name, so that we can talk about it?"

"Faces," he said.

"Faces would matter?"

"Faces would matter."

I could feel him hesitate.

"And?" I asked.

"And I can't do them. I don't have the power, the confidence, the fortitude, the commitment. I don't have what it takes. I know they would matter, but I can't manage them."

"That's a heartbreaking statement," I said.

"Yes."

"Which I don't believe for a moment."

He looked up suddenly.

"No," I continued. "You haven't tried yet. You fell into the reasonable place of making beautiful things that connected to a philosophy that attracts you. You have all the skills and heart you need — that shines through in your prints. To say that you can't do the deep work that you just named and that would matter to you is preposterous."

For the first time he laughed.

"No, you're absolutely right," he replied. "I just got afraid. That's all. To put my real dream on the table and imagine failing at it — that was too scary to contemplate." He shook his head. "But I don't need to predict failure. I don't need to think that! I know how to show up. I know how not to scare myself with bad thoughts — at least, I think I do." He smiled. "I wonder if my practice will stand up to this challenge — to do real work."

"Let's predict that it will!"

He nodded.

"So," I said, "what will you be doing?"

"Making powerful images that matter."

"Yes." I studied him for a moment. "Do we need to go over the details? How many hours a day you'll work at this — any of that?"

He shook his head. "No. I know how to work. I've just been working on the wrong things."

"Well, then! What do you want to plant in your head as your last thought for this session?"

He thought. "That I have work to do — and not just any work, because I've always worked. My job is to do this *real* work."

"I believe I can let you go on that note," I said.

He smiled, thanked me, and left.

My Wife Has the Problem

Jake, a would-be filmmaker in his early thirties, came to see me.

"How are you doing?" I asked.

"I'm good. I'm pushing along with my film — it's getting there. It's my wife...she has the problem."

"What's that?"

"The film is going to cost a lot. And we're spending our own money on it. The money we'd saved as a down payment for a house."

"She isn't on board with that idea?"

"She hates it. We've had hellacious fights."

"I don't think I'd be too happy either!" I laughed. "But you seem to have made up your mind. About the film versus your relationship."

"No! It isn't like that at all —"

"You're not holding the film as more important than the relationship?"

"No!" he said excitedly. "If she could just see where this will lead . . . how good this will be for both of us."

I nodded. "You want her to change her mind and get on board with an open heart?"

"Yes!"

"While you're spending the down payment for the house she wants. Did she save that money?" I asked.

He didn't reply. "Part of it came from a small inheritance I got," he finally blurted out. "This film could win an Academy Award!"

It's hard not to be self-interested — or selfish. With the proliferation of reality shows, we are getting a very nice education in the grandiosity and selfishness of people, whether they are celebrity hairdressers, chefs, or real estate agents. Arrogant, narcissistic, defensive, combative — we are getting an eyeful. It was going to be interesting to see to what extent Jake had a conscience and some character.

"You've tried to find outside funding?" I asked.

He shook his head. "That's way too hard! We have the money and we have credit cards and I can borrow more from my parents if need be — I can keep it all right inside our family and get the film done without having to go around begging."

"Begging?"

He made a face. "That's what it feels like!"

"You've tried it?"

"No." He hesitated. "I wouldn't even know where to begin."

"So it seems easier to spend your down payment than to investigate funding?"

"I don't feel like you're really on my side," he said, shifting uneasily.

"Why? Because I think your wife's concerns also matter?"

He got up abruptly and walked around the room. Finally he sat back down.

"I don't think you understand the upside of this project. Everybody I tell about the concept loves it."

"So tell me," I said. "How much of the movie is made?"

"I have a rough draft of the script. A rough draft of most of the script — half at least."

I nodded. "But you've already spent a lot of money?"

"On equipment. You need the right equipment. And I paid to have an original score composed — that's been a mess! And I hired someone to scout locations. There are a lot of expenses before you can actually get started!"

I nodded. "Absolutely. But I'm trying to understand your approach to this. Why commission an original score when money is tight?"

He threw up his hands. "I could hear just the right music in my head. But the composer I hired didn't really get it."

I took a breath.

"Okay," I said. "Let me make sure I'm getting this right. Are you saying that you're having problems making this movie, or are you just having problems getting your wife's buy-in?"

He shook his head. "Well, it's very complicated making a movie, and this is my first one. And I got off on the wrong foot with the composer and with this editor I hired to look at my partial script. And I was supposed to get better tech support on the equipment I bought — that's been kind of a nightmare. But I just wish my wife was in this with me. She keeps nagging me, and I can't concentrate on getting the script finished."

"A lot of relationship problems," I said.

He shrugged. "I just need people to do what they say. That's all."

"Your wife said that she would support you in this?"

"She did! In the beginning. I told her about my dream when we first met, and she was gung ho. Then some years passed while I was working on the script, and she changed her tune. She was all for it in the beginning!"

"Things changed."

"My dream didn't!"

We continued on in this vein. I renewed my wonder about the possibility and reasonableness of hunting for outside funding — not interested. I wondered if it made sense not to spend more money until he had a viable script ready — not possible. I wondered if there was any way his wife could get her house and he could get his film — no. I put on the table the question of whether he had entered into clear agreements with the composer, the location scout, the editor, the tech support people — of course he had. Everything was fine, if only his wife would second the motion.

Some of the silences grew very long. He had less to say — he knew what I was thinking. He knew that I was thinking that *he* had the problem. He couldn't wait to leave. Finally our time was up and he got his wish. We did not set up a second appointment.

Years ago I worked with court-mandated clients who had to return even after I confronted them — but no court had sent Jake to see me. Unlike those court-mandated clients, Jake was free to make his movie and disrespect his wife. I didn't expect to see Jake again — or his movie.

The Art of Relationship

Continue your investigation of right relating by answering the following questions:

- What are the key relationships in your life?
- What are the key relationships in your *creative* life?
- What additional relationships would you like to cultivate for the sake of your creative life?
- How will you go about finding advocates and supporters of your creative work?
- Where would you like to improve in your relating?
- Most crucial, how will you go about making those improvements?

Chapter 8

THE IDENTITY KEY

In this chapter we'll look at the rich and complex idea of identity and how it relates to your quest for your best life in the arts.

Consider the following two headlines. First, it is much harder to fashion a life in the arts if you do not strongly identify as an artist. Second, a vast array of subidentities is available to you — you may decide to see yourself as a beautifier, an activist, a bohemian, a problem solver, a shaman — and this array has real value to you. You'll see what I mean as we proceed.

Let's begin with seven core ideas about identity:

1. *Our identities are made up of many self-identifications that in any given person might include Jew, painter, Bostonian, woman, and on and on.* But we are different from and bigger than all those self-identifications.

The concept of "identity" is not equivalent to the concept of "self." To make a metaphor out of it, "self" is that inner Cartesian stage in which everything we think and feel plays itself out; *some* of the things that play themselves out are our self-identifications. We can step back from our sense of identity and *decide* how we want to identify ourselves.

2. *We don't know and can't know which of our self-identifications are hardwired into us and which arise by a combination of happenstance and affinity.* It seems likely that our sexual orientation is hardwired into us, but is being a Jew or a Christian? It seems even less likely that anyone is hardwired to be a Bostonian or a New Yorker. But what about being a writer, painter, filmmaker, or musician? If by some chance a self-identification like that is hardwired into us, then we are going to feel miserable not doing that work, just as we would feel miserable not pursuing our sexual preferences because of cultural injunctions. On the other hand, if being a writer, painter, filmmaker, or musician is "just" a matter of happenstance and affinity, then it would run much less deep than something like sexual preference and, by running less deep, need a lot of work to manifest and maintain. Let me repeat this point simply: if being a writer is hardwired in you, you are going to feel bad not writing; and if it isn't hardwired in you, then you are going to have to pay attention to it so that it doesn't recede or even vanish.

3. *This means that if we aren't writing and we feel the need to write — if, that is, when we're not writing, something in us feels off or missing — that may mean that writing is somehow hardwired into us and we are forcibly ignoring it, or it may mean that our writer identity is circumstantial and real but too weak to manifest itself.* In either case, the answer is to write. Let me repeat this

point simply: If we feel that we should be writing (or painting or filmmaking or composing) and we aren't writing, we may be negatively affecting our mental health by not taking one of our identity pieces seriously enough. If by not writing you are denying your identity, that can't be good for your emotional health.

4. *The identity you manifest is significantly influenced by circumstance.* Your self-identification as a Jew will come forward when you read a book about peace in the Middle East and recede when you read a book about flowers of the Northwest. You read the former as a Jew, so to speak, but you read the latter as a botanist, as a painter, or just as a human being. This is a very important point, because it means that in most situations you will react out of one of your primary self-identifications, reacting as a woman first, or as a Jew first, or as an African American first, or as a mother first; and your artist identity may not make itself felt in that moment unless you are very accustomed to leading with that identity.

5. *It follows from the previous points that it is on your shoulders to nurture and pay attention to your artist identity.* That identity can't take care of itself. To put it in simple terms, if you intend to keep writing over the long haul, day in and day out and year in and year out, you will need to strengthen your identity as a writer. Shortly we'll look at ways of doing exactly that.

6. *At first glance this point seems a bit contradictory to the last point: we want to strongly identify as human beings.* That is, different from and apart from all our individual self-identifications, we need a strong self that serves as our executive and that is separate from and larger than any self-identification. Our primary identity needs to be that of human being rather than that of Jew, painter, Bostonian, woman, and so on,

because it is only as a complete person that we can know what we value and what meaning we intend to make. To make a small joke of it, letting the Bostonian in you decide where you will live means that you have no chance of ever leaving Boston. You want to make decisions of that sort as a whole person, not from a part of your self that is rooting for a certain outcome.

7. *Related to the last two points, you must learn how to fully inhabit an identity when that serves you and also how to detach from that identity when doing so serves you better.* You fully inhabit the identity of writer when you want to write, and you fully inhabit the identity of a complete person when you want to make a moral judgment or a life decision. If you let yourself overinvest in any given self-identification, you veer toward unhealthy narcissism, as with the writers of yesteryear who felt no shame in saying things like "I don't care how hard my wife has to work or how many people I exploit, just as long as I get my novel written." Yes, you want to inhabit your artist identity; but you mustn't forget that you are a human being first and foremost *before* you are an artist.

Strengthening Your Identity as an Artist

To repeat, you want to lead your life as a whole person. You also want to strongly identify as the artist you intend to be. Here, then, are ten tips for strengthening your identity as an artist, using as our example the identity of filmmaker:

1. *Get in the habit of saying, "I am a filmmaker."* Just as it is powerful and useful for an alcoholic to say, "I am an alcoholic" out loud at an AA meeting, it is likewise powerful and useful for a filmmaker, even one who

hasn't yet made any films, to say both internally and publicly, "I am a filmmaker."

When someone asks you what you do, you say, "I'm a filmmaker with a day job" rather than "I sell shoes at Macy's." There is a world of difference between these two ways of identifying yourself: the first allows you to think about film, talk about film, network about film, and be a filmmaker; the second does no such thing.

2. *If you want to strengthen your identity as a filmmaker, ask yourself, "What does it mean to be a filmmaker?" or "What do I mean when I say that I'm a filmmaker?"* The first and obvious answer will be "Well, it means that I make films!" But it also means many other things, from, for instance, reading books about how independent films are financed to taking trips that allow you to visit interesting film festivals. Sit down and ascertain what being a filmmaker means to you.

3. *Prepare answers to the questions that, when put to you, cause you to lose your will to call yourself a filmmaker.* One such question might be "Have you made any films yet?" A second question might be "Would I have heard of any of your films?" A third question might be "Do you have to finance your films yourself — are they the equivalent of self-publishing or vanity publishing?"

Maybe, because you make shorts that are ten or twenty minutes long, being asked, "How long are your films?" causes you to sink. Bravely articulate the questions that bother you, embarrass you, weaken you, or stop you — and create answers. For instance, to the question "Have you made any films yet?," your prepared answer might be "I'm working on one right now on the theme of immigration — care to invest in it?"

4. *Do the various things that a filmmaker does.* This

means more than just "make films." It means understanding how films get made from both a technical and a financial standpoint. It means forming working relationships with people who can help you. It means learning to use language in rhetorically strong ways so that you make your films sound interesting to investors and audiences. It means understanding how to audition actors and how to work with casting directors. It means wooing rich people and learning how to negotiate with the moneyed class. It means engaging in apprenticeship activities that serve you. These are the sorts of things that filmmakers do — and to solidify your self-identification as a filmmaker, you want to do them too.

5. *Create opportunities to be a filmmaker.* In school, opportunities are regularly created for students to make and show films. Then, once you graduate, those ready-made opportunities vanish, and you must enter the real world. In the real world, you must create your opportunities to make films, efforts that might include choosing a project with a lot of appeal, getting your script or storyboard done quickly, inviting friends to invite their friends to help with the financing, and using Internet fund-raising sites to raise money. The shorthand for all this is: work. Making a film is work, but creating the *opportunity* to make that film is work as well.

6. *Seize the opportunities given to you to be a filmmaker.* If someone says, "I'm looking for an assistant director on my next film," you can respond with anxiety by saying, "Oh, I'm not ready for that!," you can respond with stubborn pride, "Oh, no, it's director or nothing for me!," or you can ask for details and see if this opportunity serves you. If you judge that it might, seize it. You want to incline yourself toward

accepting opportunities rather than rejecting them, just as long as you have tried your best to judge the viability of the project and the professionalism of the players involved.

7. *Notice if and when your filmmaker identity begins to weaken or vanish.* This happens most characteristically when you've spent too much time not operating as a filmmaker: that is, as the months go by and you neither plan nor make films. During those sad months it is entirely likely that you will begin to think of yourself less and less as a filmmaker. You want to notice that this is happening, even though it is painful to notice, and admit to yourself that your identity is eroding.

8. *Know what to do when your identity of filmmaker begins to weaken or vanish.* What will your game plan be? It can't be to instantly make a full-length movie: you don't have that sort of control over life. Nor should it be "I think I'll watch a few movies," an effort that is completely in your control but doesn't sufficiently strengthen your identity of filmmaker. It might be to turn over your morning creativity practice to getting your script written; it might be to start to engage in three fund-raising efforts daily; it might be to reconnect with those folks who have shown a little interest in you as a filmmaker and remake their acquaintance. You want a game plan in place so that when your identity of filmmaker weakens you'll know exactly what useful things you can do.

9. *Know what to do when you think you've lost your right to call yourself a filmmaker because you haven't made a film in five years, because your last film was roundly panned, or because you have to pay for making your films yourself.* None of these events should lose you your right to call yourself a filmmaker — that will

happen only if you let it happen. When you feel as if you've lost that right, what will you do? At the very least, resume saying, "I am a filmmaker!" internally and publicly. Know *exactly* what you are going to do when you feel your right to call yourself a filmmaker slipping away.

10. *Make the support of your artist identity something like a practice by paying daily attention to it, maybe in your morning meaning check-in or maybe in some other way.* You want daily contact with that identity, you want to know daily whether or not you are manifesting your artist identity, and if you aren't manifesting it, you want to take some action to manifest it on that very day. Naturally, you want to *be* a filmmaker every day, but equally important, you want to *support your identity* of filmmaker every day. There may be days when you don't work on your film, but there should be no days when you don't feel like a filmmaker.

Your Whole Self and Your Artist Self

What is the relationship between your whole self and your artist self? This is a tremendously important subject because you want your whole self to be the monitor for all your self-identifications — Jew, woman, Bostonian, painter — so that you don't become drawn in directions you don't want to go just because something happens that pulls at one of those self-identifications.

Consider the following seven points:

1. *You are a whole person who is also an artist.* You need to maintain an important primary relationship between you as a whole person and you as an artist, so that the "whole you" is in charge and keeps an eye on all your

self-identifications, just as a third-grade teacher might mind her eight-year-olds.

To take a simple example, your writer identity may be hungry to do something fun, but your whole self may understand that you have a book to write that is more important than the fun book but also more like sheer slogging work than enjoyment. You want your whole self deciding these matters, just as you would want the teacher and not the eight-year-olds running the class.

2. *Next is the matter of keeping your eye on your values and principles.* Your artist identity may want to make meaning in a certain way, say, by using some Native American imagery in your next suite of paintings. But your whole self may have something to say about the rightness or value of expropriating imagery from another culture.

You may want to paint something because it strikes you as arresting or beautiful, but you still want your whole self to ask the question "Are there other considerations here besides beauty?" You might think of this as mind monitoring heart or as conscience monitoring ego, but probably the best way to think of it is as your whole self monitoring your artist self. If your whole self is monitoring your artist self, then you will make not only meaning but *value-based* meaning.

3. *There is an important difference between monitoring your self-identifications, which is a good thing, and using this idea of identity as yet another way not to get on with your creative work.* I think you can see how you might use this executive function idea as a way to doubt yourself or your current creative project. Say that you've decided to abstract some pine trees into geometric shapes, and let's say your first results aren't all that pleasing to you. Using this idea of whole self

monitoring artist self, you might say to yourself, "Gee, I wonder if abstracting these pine trees is really a valuable idea?" and cast the whole project in doubt.

In some instances this may be a proper question, but very often — maybe most often — it will just be a reaction to difficulty and a way to avoid the pain of process. Do not use this idea of monitoring as a way to avoid hard work or as a way to evade the realities of process.

4. *Running a bit counter to the previous points, you want to strongly hold and cherish those self-identifications that you want to hold and cherish, like the identity of artist.* Sometimes you'll have to tell your whole self, "Hey, self, I know I'm obsessing a lot about this novel and writing day and night, but please don't bug me about my 'whole self' right now — I need to be writing!"

Usually you will lead with your whole self but sometimes you will want to honor and give free rein to your artist self, so it follows that these inner relationships will produce real conflicts — and conflicts generate anxiety. This means that you will want to have your anxiety-management tools at the ready to deal with these identity issues, because as abstract as they may seem in this discussion, they are very real and will cause real conflicts in your being.

5. *Just as the tension between your whole self and your various self-identifications produces anxiety, the following dynamic does as well.* Your whole self is not a static entity, and neither are your self-identifications. This ongoing shifting and changing causes discomfort and uncertainty, because somewhere in our minds we presume or hope that we have "settled down by now" into some stable something — and we sense that we haven't.

There is really no reason to suppose that we will ever settle down in this way, not as long as life presents us with new experiences and not as long as we ourselves desire to grow and change. Expect this regular shifting of identity, and when it comes, have your anxiety-management tools ready so you can deal with the anxiety such shifting naturally provokes.

6. *When you learn how to operate from your whole self, rather than reacting in a knee-jerk way from one or another of your many self-identifications, you will also learn how to choose which identity piece to respond from.* Your whole self has that executive function.

To take a simple example, let's say that a bit of news about some event in the Middle East stirs and exasperates you. You can react as a Jew, you can react as a pacifist, you can react as a mother, you can react as a poet, but the starting place is to invite your whole self to consider the situation and to express its opinion about which self-identification it wants to nominate. To put it in everyday language, you can decide whether you want to react to the situation as a poet, as a Jew, as a mother, and so on. Honoring this capability is the same thing as making value-based meaning.

7. *Seventh and last, this matter of operating from your whole self rather than from any given identity piece is quite significant, because if you fall into the trap of operating too completely or too permanently from one identity piece or another, you may lock yourself into a certain smallness — even if, for example, you get a tremendous amount of painting or writing done.*

This is why many highly productive artists also seem immature and incomplete. They have given their artist identify free and full rein and have lost out by not paying sufficient attention to their whole self with its executive-functioning capabilities and its ability to look at the whole story.

Remember: you don't want to put all your eggs in the basket of any identity piece, even the identity piece of artist. You will remember from our previous discussion how important I think it is that you strengthen your identity as an artist in order to give yourself the chance to *be* that artist. Here I am saying, *do* strengthen that identity piece and really feel that you are an artist and really live as an artist *but* at the same time recognize that you have a whole self that is larger than and different from your identity as an artist.

Let me summarize: 1) We possess many self-identifications and many identity pieces. 2) One of them is the identity of artist, and we want to nurture and strengthen that identity piece so that we can be the artist we want to be. 3) We do not want to strengthen the identity piece of artist in such a way that we fail to live life as a whole person.

Adopting a Public Persona

The large question we've touched on in this chapter is "How will you shape your identity?" A second, equally important question is "Who will you be in public?"

The answers to these questions do not have to be the same! You can be much more your "real self" in private and as you create, and rather more of a construction when you operate out in the world, a place of conventions and obligations.

To what extent ought you to be your real self in your public interactions? Think of the elementary school teacher who would love to smile but who has learned that to maintain order in her classroom, she must adopt a certain stern attitude until December. She would love to smile, but she knows better. Like the teacher, you may have very good reasons to adopt a public persona that is different from your everyday or in-studio persona.

There are two ways to think about your public persona. One is that adopting a public persona is a way to practice doing better in public than you typically do in private. You might craft a public persona that allows you to exhibit more confidence than you actually feel, to be clear when in your own mind you feel fuzzy, or to ask pointed questions that you might let slip if you were having a conversation with only yourself. In this sense your public persona can reflect the changes that you would like to make to your personality: in this example, you would actually like to be this more assertive, clearer person.

On the other hand, maybe you are quite happy with who you are in private but recognize that your irony does not play well in public, that your frankness tends to be received as brusqueness, and that the qualities you take pride in have to be modulated in a public setting. In that case, you can create a strategic public persona that matches what the world wants and allows you to interact effectively with customers, collectors, framers, gallery owners, and media representatives.

In the first instance, you are using your public persona both strategically and to improve yourself, and in the second, improvement may not be a goal, but strategic self-presentation certainly is.

If you are not paying attention to the difference between what is required of you in public and what you can permit yourself in private, you are likely to present yourself ineffectively in the marketplace. Indeed, these dynamics are often played out in our artist statements. Many artist statements are abrupt and downright rude, demanding that if the viewer doesn't "get" the painting, she should immediately take herself to a remedial "What is art?" class. The artist's resentments, disappointments, and grandiosity spill out into his statement, making for a missive that the artist would call frank but that a viewer knows is combative and defensive.

Just as unfortunate, many artists' statements have that vague, mind-numbingly abstract quality, so that the artist could be talking about any work or no work. A viewer can't help but presume that such a statement mirrors the artist's indecisive, unconfident inner reality. The artist's intelligence, wit, and humanity do not show through, and all the viewer is left with — regardless of the actual imagery on display — is a stifled yawn.

In both cases the artist has not made a sufficient effort to do the inner work that would result in personality growth on the one hand and the creation of an appropriate public persona on the other.

Donna, a painter, explained, "Whether by nature or nurture, I am a shy person who prefers to spend her time in the studio and who will do almost anything to avoid marketplace interactions. This way of being suited me better when I was learning my craft, since I really did need to focus on what was going on in the studio. But now that I have a body of work — an overflowing body of work — I need to step out into the world in ways that I find strange and uncomfortable. I have to make myself do it — it does not come naturally. I actually have a checklist of the qualities that I want to manifest that I keep by the computer, so that every email I send out is coming from my public persona and not my shy studio personality."

Steven, a sculptor, reported, "I've been in recovery for eight years now. Before that, when I was actively drinking, I always led with my temper. I had an attacking style — I would interrupt you, contradict you, fight you over every detail and the smallest perceived grievance, and always get in the last word. I was angry all the time, which was maybe a good thing with respect to the sculptures, since they had a lot of angry energy to them, but which was not good anywhere else in my life. Over these eight years of recovery, I've cultivated a way of being that is more temperate, centered, and essentially gentle. Actually, I'm really still as hard as nails, and people really ought not to cross me; but that part of me is kept under lock and key and almost never appears in public."

An artist's public persona is a thoughtful, measured presentation of the artist as she puts forward those qualities that she has identified as serving her best in the public arena. What qualities would you like to lead with in your public interactions? How would you like to be perceived? What public persona would allow you to advocate for your work most effectively? Build that persona and try it out — in public, naturally!

The Evidence of Your Eyes

Frances had come to narrative painting late in life, after twenty years as a corporate lawyer. Her paintings were large and powerful, and they sold well. But she had the hardest time not bad-mouthing them, both during the full four months it took her to paint one and after each was done.

"I think I want a different way of working," she said in our first session. "I want to paint more loosely; I want to paint more quickly — four months on one of these paintings almost kills me!"

I smiled. "Yes, maybe it would be nice if the process were a little less painful. Not pain free — that might be too much to ask. But just a little less painful?"

"I need to get the details right," she proceeded, not quite listening. "So, there I am, working on this or that detail, and while I'm working on the detail the whole thing seems dead to me. I keep asking myself, 'What's the point?' and 'Who would want this?' and 'Is this any good?' I might spend a whole day painting a hand, getting it right, and that whole day I'm bitching to myself."

I nodded. "Is part of it coming to painting later in life?"

"Probably," she said. "But how do you mean?"

"If you felt that you were born to paint and had been draw-ing and painting forever, you might doubt a given painting but not doubt *yourself* so much. It sounds like you aren't just doubting the painting in front of you but doubting whether you're an artist."

She answered instantly. "I do doubt that! I don't have any confidence that I am an artist."

"Even though people buy your paintings? Even though people praise them? Even though you yourself respect them — when you aren't bad-mouthing them?"

She shrugged. "People buy stupid things all the time, things of no value. That my paintings sell doesn't prove much to me. The praise — well, I don't know that I respect the peo-ple who praise my work all that much. And as for my own opinions — I guess I am deeply not sure whether or not I respect them."

I wanted to whistle. That was a lot of doubting!

"Let's come at it from a slightly different angle," I said. "What would be different if you started each painting from the sure place that you were an artist? If you were always say-ing to yourself, 'I have no doubt that I'm an artist, no matter how my current painting is going'?"

She thought about that. "I think it would actually make a huge difference. I would have — *faith* is probably the word — faith that the painting had a chance of turning out well. As opposed to my current mind-set, which is that it really has no chance. It would make a huge difference." She glanced at me. "But of course I would have to believe it — just saying it wouldn't mean much. I'm not into fooling myself."

"So, it would be nice if you believed that you were an art-ist. We both agree on that. But sales of your paintings won't convince you of that, praise won't convince you of that, and looking at your paintings doesn't convince you of that. What would?"

"The looking part. If, when I looked at a painting of mine, I could honestly say, 'I'm satisfied with that.'"

"And sometimes you are able to say that?"

"Yes. But then I don't trust my own judgment."

"So, let me see if I've got it. You can't call yourself an artist unless what you see in front of you convinces you that you are an artist, but even when what you see in front of you seems to prove that you are an artist, you still doubt your eyes. Does that sound like a fair paraphrase?"

She sat thinking. "It does."

"Then you see the problem, yes?"

She nodded after a bit. "I may be very talented at doubting what I see in front of me. In which case I may never be able to say, 'Aha, there's the proof!' It may be right there, but I might refuse to accept it."

We sat quietly.

"You can see the sort of chicken-and-egg problem we have," I said. "You can't say that you're an artist until your eyes confirm it — and your eyes may never confirm it."

"Even if the proof is right there in front of me," she said thoughtfully.

She had a lot to think about. I let her think. I could imagine her train of thought. Doubtless she would keep circling back to a couple of questions: "Is my work good, or isn't it?" and "Compared to what?" and "How can I know?"

"I could, as a linguistic matter, start to say 'I am an artist,'" she finally said. "As a kind of affirmation or wish — or prophecy. Even if I didn't believe it—"

"Maybe. That's possible. But I'd like you to try something different — something more ambitious," I said, smiling. "It's a change in your vision of the truth of the matter. I would like you to really believe something that I know you sometimes believe — that you are an artist." I paused. "You do sometimes believe that?"

"I do."

"And then you talk yourself out of that belief?"

"Exactly."

"That's what needs to stop happening."

How odd to have to arm-wrestle someone who was obviously an artist into the belief that she was an artist! What powerful reasons must be involved in her refusal! I waited. She couldn't quite get there. I could see the frustration in her eyes. She couldn't convince herself that she was an artist.

"All right," I said. "Let's go the other route. The linguistic one."

"And fake it until I make it."

"Exactly. You will now begin to say 'I am an artist' as an affirmation and prophecy."

She nodded.

"Whether or not what you see on the canvas convinces you."

She nodded.

"As a way of opening the door to what I wish you already could acknowledge, that you are an artist."

She couldn't nod to this. But she didn't turn away from it either.

Your Artist Identity

In this chapter I've tried to tease out some of the more important ideas about identity. If you'd like to continue this exploration, answer the following questions:

- What are your primary self-identifications (man, Baptist, American, Republican)?
- Is "real artist" one of your primary self-identifications?
- What do you think is the importance (or lack of importance) of self-identifying as a "real artist"?
- What in-studio identity do you want to cultivate and adopt?
- What public persona do you want to craft and present?

Let's tie a few of these ideas together. You will feel more confident (the confidence key) if you strongly identify as an artist. You will experience less stress (the stress key) if you use your executive function to make strong, smart decisions about how you intend to identify yourself. You will do a better job of relating (the relationship key) once you realize that you can craft and hone a public persona of your own choosing. Even though "identity" is an abstract idea, it has tremendous real-world consequences and applications. It will benefit you to take some time and sit with the puzzle that is your identity.

Chapter 9

THE SOCIETAL KEY

Every contemporary creative person is embedded in a complex society in which she lives, learns her life lessons, and tries to sell her wares. She learns what is acceptable and what is not; she comes to understand what most people around her find entertaining; she learns her society's conventions and idiosyncrasies.

She knows exactly what the phrase *white picket fence* connotes and what buttons will be pushed by words like *welfare* and *abortion*. Whether or not she knows it, she measures every conversation she has and every action she takes against the consequences she expects from violating the rules of her society.

How artists are affected by and react to their society is an enormous topic. Let's focus on one corner of this vast territory: self-censorship. Most of us assume that we are free to think just about anything and to express ourselves in any way we see fit. In reality, artists do a lot of measuring, somewhere just out of conscious awareness, about what is safe or seemly to reveal and what is not.

They decide to set their novel in a foreign country because they do not feel safe talking about the evildoers in their hometown. They paint lively abstractions or cheerful landscapes because they fear what Goyaesque horrors might escape from their brush in a narrative painting. When a nonfiction idea begins to percolate in their brain, an idea that if published might cause the government to retaliate, they find reasons to dismiss the project. We all do these sorts of things.

We are talking about the most primitive and important of motives here, our personal safety and survival, and why, because of the power of these motives, so many artists and would-be artists practice ongoing self-censorship. One aspect of this self-censorship is the way we bite our tongue at our day job and, in a corollary safety measure, skip making art that reveals what our corporation, institution, or agency is up to. We don't tell tales out of school about the school where we work; we don't reveal the dirt about the police department that employs us; we don't portray our madcap board of directors in our novel or paint a Kafkaesque likeness of our governmental agencies.

These knotty psychological and practical matters confront virtually every artist. Here is one report from a writer and performance artist in England, Louise:

"I have decided to quit my job as an art psychotherapist in the National Health Service after seven long years. I worked in a big psychiatric hospital with in-patients, out-patients, acutely distressed people, psychotic clients, people with personality disorders and alcohol problems, and suicidal people. When I was younger I could never have imagined becoming part of the mental health system, since I always thought there was something intrinsically wrong and bad with a system that still depends so strongly on the medical model. But I found myself with a job within a flourishing and lively art-therapy department, and for years I was quite happy there, seeing that good work could be done within this system.

"But I have gone right back to my previous position. I now think that our department has been systematically destroyed over the past two and a half years, that we're only a shadow of our former selves, that we've lost all our autonomy due to 'institutional restructuring' (what a ridiculous phrase for such a violent process!), and it has become impossible for me to work there and still feel good about myself. One scary issue for me has been to see how I have felt silenced, just like my clients, by a system that in the end really only cares about economics and personal power.

"I have not yet worked directly with the outrage I feel about all this in my writing or my performance art, maybe because I have a feeling that I need to gain some distance in order to speak again, to find my voice again. I am German, and only when I moved to Britain twelve years ago did I start to slowly find a voice about the shame and guilt that I brought with me because of my German heritage. Now, twelve years later, I have Jewish friends and I am taking a performance piece on tour in which I honestly, humorously, courageously, and deeply speak about my experiences of being German here and about my outrage, shame, and deep sadness about the wounds of history. All this has finally found a voice. And I have a feeling that my next piece will be very much about my journey within the mental health system, my strange position within it. I am sad that I need the distance in order to really speak out, but better to speak at some point than never at all!"

Can an artist manage to live inside his society while at the same time daring to tell the truth about it? Or will he invariably be punished and exiled if he tells uncomfortable truths? One television satirist becomes a huge star for excoriating the sitting president, while another satirist becomes a pariah for telling the same truths. A museum puts on a well-attended show of Goya prints that point out the sins of capitalism, and yet no gallery within miles of that museum will touch contemporary prints on the same subject. How is an artist to calculate the odds that he will remain safe if he tells the truth or, if he courageously tells that truth, that he will garner any sort of audience?

An artist is right to feel confused and uncertain as to what will happen to him if and when he decides to censor himself less. You may do creative work in which this seems not to be an issue — say, basic biological research or cheerful watercolors — but funding for the former is connected to the politics of your society, and your interest in the latter may be more a flight away from dark material than an actual desire to paint cheerfully. Creative individuals owe it to themselves to ask and try to answer these two questions: "Am I doing the creative work I intend to do?" and "If I'm not, is self-censorship the issue?"

The Role of the Artist in Society

Artists are embedded in society. If we think about how artists have historically viewed themselves as functioning in their society and how they've positioned themselves in society, we see many different models. Let's consider a dozen of them. As we proceed, think about which of these roles might be a match for you.

In each case I'll use as an example a painter whose subject matter is flowers, to give you a sense of how artists who opt for a similar subject matter may nevertheless be maintaining a completely different relationship with society.

1. *The classical artist aimed for technical excellence and formal beauty.* "My art speaks to universals. I intend to paint beautiful flowers regardless of what is going on in society. Maybe my beautiful flowers will heal

people who are harmed, maybe my flowers will bring a smile to the faces of people who are sad, but such outcomes are just happy unintended consequences of what I do. I am not looking for any outcomes in society — I am simply doing the art that speaks to me and to my sense of what is unchanging, eternal, and universal."

2. *The medieval artist aimed for a certain kind of anonymity and service.* "One of the subjects that my guild employs to praise God and one of the subjects we use to decorate holy sites is the flower. Therefore I have apprenticed in the art of flower painting to a master flower painter, and I am humbly and rigorously learning my craft. When I learn it I will become one of many who serve by painting flowers."

3. *The Renaissance artist wanted his name known and sported an individual ego and individual ambitions.* "My flowers are special and, frankly, a work of real genius. They may praise God, but it's important to me that people know my name and recognize my uniqueness and my greatness."

4. *The court artist resided inside society's most powerful inner circle and was beholden to and a plaything of the powerful.* "The queen is attracted to lilies, but the king hates them. So although I am painting my next painting for the queen, I nevertheless must finesse her out of her desire for lilies and sell her on something that won't upset the king. But I better not upset her either! — because she too can lop off my head!"

5. *The society artist played a similar game to the court artist, only inside the world of the wealthy and the privileged instead of the regal.* "I can't wait for the Smiths to see my new chrysanthemum painting that the Joneses just put up! With luck, I can spend all summer at the

Smiths' place on the island painting them a chrysanthemum or two."

6. *The revolutionary artist stood as a witness to her society and adopted the stance of activist.* "I am going to
paint a series of flower paintings in which each flower
is a martyr executed by our fascistic government. By
using flowers as my motif I'll be able to speak to the
bourgeoisie, who would never listen if I painted fir-
ing squads like Goya. My flowers will help foment the
coming revolution!"

7. *The bohemian artist thumbed her nose at society and
burned her candle at both ends.* "Having been high
for nine days now, I have some truly amazing flowers
popping out of the psychedelic haze that is my life. As
soon as I finish this Scotch and stumble my way to the
canvas, I will express with great poetry and passion
the flowers that are crawling under my skin."

8. *The modern artist aimed for progress and innovation.*
"Most people will not understand what I'm doing
when I turn the common red rose into a blue abstrac-
tion, but artists will understand, some segments of
society will eventually understand, and in the process
I will have moved art forward from its sad past as dec-
oration and plaything for the rich."

9. *The contemporary global artist can position herself
broadly, worldwide, so to speak.* "I have been painting
here in Hong Kong for five years now, but my large-
scale flower paintings do not fit the cultural norms
or aesthetic idiom I find here in Hong Kong. So I am
picking up and moving to Florence, where my flowers
will strike a chord with a society brought up on and
surrounded by Renaissance floral painting."

10. *The mass-market artist is interested in large-scale success and in reaching the most people possible, whether
with a hit television show, a hit book, or a hit CD.* "I'm

going to finesse my way onto that new reality show where twenty people live together in a glass house and do my darnedest to become the villain on that show, since becoming the fan favorite isn't in my nature. By the end of that series the whole world will be wanting my flower paintings — which I'll hire some people to paint while I'm toiling away in that glass house becoming a celebrity."

11. *The small-business artist is functionally like any shopkeeper on any village street, hand-selling her poetry chapbooks, scented candles, homemade CDs, and watercolors — in cyberspace as well as in brick-and-mortar outlets.* "I'm going to paint the idiosyncratic flowers I want to paint, put up an attractive website, and market to those members of society who might take an interest in what I paint. I'm going to create my cyberspace presence and see who comes along to shop."

12. *The contemporary postmodern artist is awash in competing choices, competing roles, competing metaphors, and competing narratives.* "This month I'm doing installation flowers that speak to my sense of isolation and alienation from society, but at the same time I want to do a coffee-table book of flower paintings that is partly ironic and also just simply beautiful, and at the same time I want to deconstruct the flower and move it way past what Mondrian ever did."

In one form or another all these roles are still available to today's artist. There is a way to be a classical artist, a way to be a medieval artist, a way to be a society artist. Most artists will probably find themselves falling into one or another of the last two categories — that is, most will become small-business artists who try to hand-sell to those segments of society that appreciate them or will become postmodern artists whose relationship to society changes frequently and even abruptly.

But while most artists will probably find themselves in one or another of the last two categories, it's important to remember that all these categories continue to exist in their own ways, and that it will pay you enormous dividends to think through what relationship you want to fashion with your culture and your society.

Choosing Your Role in Society

Most artists never think through how they want to relate to their society or what role they want to adopt as artists. Rather, they accidentally fall into one role or another or into one relationship or another.

Let's say that you want to prove the exception and mindfully choose your relationship to your society. Here are nine tips for doing just that:

1. *Think through the many roles available to you.* If you agree that, as a general principle, gaining awareness is a large part of your job, then this is an excellent place to pay some specific attention and gain some specific awareness.

   You might run through my list of roles, or you might think the matter through in your own way and come up with some categories that you think capture the opportunities available to artists today.

   Try not to decide right off the bat which roles attract you and which ones repel you. As a first step just think through the nature and meaning of each category. You'll learn a lot just by thinking through what a contemporary classical artist might look like, what a contemporary society artist might look like, what a contemporary revolutionary artist might look like, and so on.

2. *For each role that intrigues you, think through the pros*

and cons of adopting it. Using just one as an example, let's say that the small-business artist model intrigues you. You would calmly and carefully articulate the pros and cons of being that sort of artist.

The pros might include that you can keep your distance from society and mass-market concerns and focus on those elements of society — those customers — who understand what you are doing and who want to buy what you make. Adopting this role, you could retain control of your product and your marketing efforts.

The cons might include that, just like the owner of the corner restaurant who has to come in at 4:00 AM to take deliveries and doesn't close up until midnight, this role might have you doing business all the time, including during those times you would otherwise be doing your art.

For each role that intrigues you, do this patient, difficult work — you will learn a lot about how you want to be as an artist.

3. *For each role that intrigues you, try to think through if it actually interests you or if it is resonating because of some old family messages, powerful family rules, or anything else in your history.* You may, for example, be attracted to the role of medieval artist and the idea of service but only because you had a religious upbringing that stressed service and because that religious upbringing included churches, whose atmosphere remains with you and therefore naturally makes the role of medieval artist attractive to you.

You may be attracted to a role like bohemian artist because you are still rebelling against your controlling parents; you may be attracted to a role like mass-market artist because of the messages you got at home about the importance of money. Make sure that the roles that intrigue you *actually* intrigue you and aren't calling to you just because of some old associations or dynamics.

4. *For those roles that intrigue you, think through which are likely to feel like meaning opportunities and which, even though they come with significant pluses, are unlikely to generate the experience of meaning.* For instance, the role of classical artist, with its focus on formal beauty, may speak to something in you. But as you think the matter through, you might begin to see that any art you create from that place might appeal to your aesthetic sense but leave you intellectually dissatisfied and existentially cold.

Certain roles may seem more congenial or more natural to you than others, and comfort and naturalness certainly matter. But you want to check in with yourself to make sure that the role or roles you adopt actually serve your meaning needs.

5. *For those roles that intrigue you, try to gauge which ones best match your values and principles.* You may find many reasons for choosing a role that focuses on the quality and the nature of the art you make, roles, for example, like classical artist or Renaissance artist, but when you think about it you may discover that such roles and such art do not really support your values and principles.

To put it aphoristically, you may want to be a Renaissance artist but *need* to be a revolutionary artist. You may conclude that your art must *be* the way you promote your values and your principles. On the other hand, you may decide that it's perfectly proper to be a Renaissance artist, just as long as you support worthy causes also — that is, you may decide that your art does not need to carry an activist burden. You can come to smart decisions about these matters only by thinking them through.

6. *Think through the issue of money.* You may decide that you need your art to make money and that you need to choose your artist role and your artist products based on financial calculations. Not that those calculations are at all easy to make. Which is more likely to sell: beautiful flowers or something grotesque and painful to look at? It isn't easy to answer such a question, since beautiful flowers are likely to sell more easily in general, but perhaps only at art fairs and for low prices, while grotesque art that crashes through and makes your name may make you an art scene darling.

   However, despite the reality of this complexity, you can think the matter through and see if you can tweak a role that you want to adopt so that you have a better chance at an income. For example, you might decide that a revolutionary artist can also be a mass-market artist and that you are going to figure out how to do that marrying!

7. *Make a choice.* Your choice is necessarily tentative since you don't really know if it will prove a good fit and because, as we've discussed before, genuine process involves a lot of not knowing. But you will want to commit to your choice even though you are holding it as a tentative choice. This is the same full-bodied but tentative commitment that we give to our creative projects, full-bodied because we really want to bite into them, tentative because a given project may have no life and no juice and may have to be abandoned.

   Choose a role or roles that you think will really suit you on the several levels we just identified — one that will be able to meet your meaning needs, that relates sensibly to your principles and values, one that isn't a mere shadow from the past, and so on — and tentatively and wholeheartedly commit to it.

8. *Think through what might serve as a test of the rightness of your choice.* What experiment might you try, what first steps might you take, what creative projects might you pick?

    Say, for example, that you want to try your hand at some revolutionary art to see if the role really suits you. What first step might you take as a fledgling revolutionary artist? What project might flow from that decision? Imagine, returning to our example of flower paintings, that you have always painted beautiful flowers — what will you paint now?

    Will you paint flowers in a revolutionary way? Will you paint a bouquet of flowers that's informed by revolutionary iconography? Will you change your subject matter entirely? These are the sorts of questions and challenges that naturally follow from your decision to mindfully choose your artist role and your relationship to society.

9. *Begin the process of trying out your new artist role.* Bring some energy, courage, diligence, and other strengths to this task.

    Remember that it is a process with all the attributes of process: that you won't know a lot of the time, that you will make mistakes and messes, that you will doubt what you are doing and hate what you are doing some portion of the time, that you will be elated at other times.

Having made a useful decision that may pan out beautifully does not mean that you can avoid process just because you made the right decision. All that you've done is made new hard work for yourself. Mindfully choosing your artist role

and your relationship to society is only the beginning of the
process.

Engaged Creativity and Alienation

One stance a creative person can take with respect to her
society is that of engagement. As employed by French existentialists like Sartre, engagement meant political and social
action. "Engagement is a specialized term in the Sartrean
vocabulary and refers to the process of accepting responsibility for the political consequences of one's actions," explains
the *Internet Encyclopedia of Philosophy*. "Sartre, more than
any other philosopher of the period, defended the notion of
socially responsible writing and was famous for writing scath-
ing essays condemning French policies. Sartre argued that a
socially responsible writer must address the major events of
the era, take a stance against injustice and work to alleviate
oppression."

Engagement is conscience in action. No sphere of human
life is shielded from ethics. Your conscience may require that
you say something to your father about his treatment of your
sister, that you destroy the invention you just created because
you do not trust how it will be used, that you choose a principle over a person or a person over a principle, that you
object vehemently when you hear a slur, or that you reject
an immoral lover. If you only *think about* confronting your
father, destroying your invention, or showing your lover the
door, no engagement has occurred.

If engagement is conscience in action, what, then, is engaged creativity? It is an act of engagement to fly across the
country to participate in a protest. It is an act of *engaged creativity* to fly across the country to protest and *also* to write
a protest song on the airplane. It is an act of engagement
to defend freedom of speech by protecting someone who is
speaking out. It is an act of *engaged creativity* to speak out

yourself in a painting that breaks with your usual subject matter and that tackles an issue that self-censorship had caused you to avoid.

Engagement is conscience in action. Engaged creativity is creative effort in moral service. Think how many of your creative efforts you want to be of this sort. Not all need be; but shouldn't some?

Some of those itches that you can't scratch, some of those episodes of sadness whose sources you can't identify, and some of the vague doubts you can't shake off may well have their roots in this particular dilemma: that you are caught in the cultural trance and burdened by your safety needs and not operating as an engaged artist. Often it is this lack of engagement that is most alienating to a creative person, who is "going along to get along" without quite realizing it.

Whatever relationships you manage to forge with your society and whatever role or roles you adopt as an artist, including the role of engaged artist, it's entirely likely that you will still not feel like you really fit in. Most artists, even as they try to fit in, often remain significantly alienated from their society.

They remain alienated for all the reasons we've chatted about: that they're likely to disagree with and feel the need to dispute many of their culture's values, that they intend to make their own meaning, retain their individuality, and stand for principles that their society may not be honoring, and so forth. Given that you are likely to feel alienated from your society no matter what role you adopt or what relationships you forge, the following are some tips for dealing with that alienation:

1. *You can try to focus on universals rather than on the particulars of your society.* For example, you might write a useful cautionary nonfiction book about historical threats to freedom rather than getting caught

up in the losses of freedom occurring right around you, matters about which you can take no effective action.

That is, by focusing on the universal nature of authoritarian threats to freedom and by doing a beautiful job of telling *that* story, you might do a lot of good for freedom and *also* reduce your experience of alienation by reorienting yourself away from the particulars (and the particular horrors) of your society.

2. *You might try to create some useful society.* Artists often feel moved to create writing groups, salons, and other artistic societies because, in addition to the other purposes that such groups serve, they may help an artist with her alienation issues.

How often this actually works is an open question, since the shadows that artists bring to these groups — the shadows of envy, ego, and so on — often make pleasant or useful relating difficult or even impossible. Still, organizing such a group may be worth a try, since some such artist groups have been known to serve their members beautifully.

If no such group exists in your area or if no group exists that seems to meet your needs, then you will have to create it yourself and maintain it — which of course is its own real job.

3. *You might join a group with shared affinities and let that socializing serve your need to belong.* The affinity group could be anything from an AA group to a conversational Italian club to a small-business group to a singles meet-up group to a watercolor group.

These groups will naturally bring in unfortunate aspects of the mass culture, since everyone in the group, you included, is a member of that mass culture; they will also bring in all sorts of problems associated with human beings gathering. But those challenges notwithstanding, if the group stays focused on sobriety or business-building practices or watercolor technique or whatever the group is meant to support, there is a real chance that the group may serve its members.

4. *You might decide to actively fight your society.* That is, you might fully acknowledge your alienation, credit it to the problems you see in society, and announce that your best recourse is to try to redress those wrongs as an activist artist or as an activist.

You might leap into the fray and leap *into* society, both as a matter of principle and as the way to be in society with other alienated folks who share your vision and your concerns. In this scenario, you are making the conscious decision not to throw up your hands and let the alienation win but instead to roll up your sleeves and arm-wrestle with your society.

5. *You might focus on meaning rather than on what's bothering you.* You focus on your next meaning investment and your next meaning opportunity rather than on what mood you find yourself in or on how alienated from society you feel. To put it differently, you try the cognitive tactic of announcing that alienation is no longer an issue for you because you've reframed the matter and no longer hold your relationship to your society as worth your attention.

6. *You can pinpoint and then physically move into another society that you suspect will prove less alienating.* This geographic cure might mean moving to a college town in the hopes of finding more people who share your values; relocating to a major art city like Berlin, London, or New York with the intention of plugging yourself into a vibrant, avant-garde scene; choosing a rural, bohemian locale where you imagine you can live laid back in the company of counterculture types;

or opting for a small art town like a Sedona or a Santa Fe, which you suspect possesses the twin virtues of an art scene and a liberating lifestyle. Sometimes these geographic cures work and sometimes they don't, but they are certainly worth considering.

These six are among your options for dealing with what may prove to be your abiding sense of alienation from your society. All may prove imperfect; some may serve you reasonably well; one might turn out to work beautifully for you. If you're feeling alienated, rather than writing the matter off as hopeless, consider these options — and dream up additional ones.

Out in the Cold

A woman named Sheila came to see me about a book she couldn't get written. It was a book in which she intended to take the insular, cultlike ethnic community in which she lived to task for its general small-mindedness and its cruel treatment of women. My first question was the obvious one.

"You intend to write this book and also remain in the community?"

"Funny," she said. "I've never heard the problem expressed so clearly — even in my own mind. Of course that's the issue! And the answer is, I think I've been intending to stay."

I nodded. "Because?"

She thought about that. "Because it's what I know. Because I have friends in the community. Because — if I leave it, who am I? Because I'm not sure that the bigger world is any better — I might be jumping from the frying pan into the fire. Because...well, and because of my husband."

"Where does he stand?"

"He's a true believer in our community. Which should

make him sexist and domineering, I suppose, but he isn't. Which weakens my argument."

"So part of you wonders if you believe your own premise?"

"That may be true."

We sat for a bit.

"Maybe I'm making it all up," she said finally.

"Did some event precipitate your desire to write this book?" I asked after a moment.

She nodded. "There was a woman — I knew her, but not that well. Her child was going to a community school where they taught about 'enemies' — all the people our community was supposed to watch out for. She made a stink. She said that was a crazy, backward way to be in the twenty-first century. There was an amazing backlash — all hell broke loose. Really, her life got ruined. She had to take her child and go away; her husband stayed behind."

"And telling just that story, as fact or fiction, doesn't work for you?" I wondered.

"Novels don't effect change," she replied instantly. "They don't make a difference. And I don't know her story well enough to tell it as fact, and I think I would be afraid of getting sued."

"And researching other, similar communities —"

She waved that away. "Doesn't interest me."

"And writing a memoir?"

"That's the one," she said reluctantly. "That's the one I want to write — and don't want to write."

"Because you have feelings for the people in the community? Or because you don't want all hell to break out in your life?"

"A little of both."

"Let's look at it the other way around. How would it be not to write about it?"

She thought about that. "I'd feel unethical. I'd be disappointing myself — I wouldn't feel proud."

We sat with that.

"Let's run through all the ways such a book might be written," I said, "and see if there are any approaches we've missed."

We did that, although she didn't have her heart in it. It seemed that she had already decided that she couldn't or wouldn't write this book — that the consequences would be too grave. We talked about screenplays, stage plays, nonfiction books of one sort, nonfiction books of another sort. We revisited the territory of fiction and memoir. We discussed blog posts, articles, even poetry. She paid only cursory attention.

"I'm guessing the form isn't the issue," I said. "The issue is, is it worth taking the risk?"

"Yes — and it isn't."

"You've decided?"

"I guess I have decided. I didn't know I'd decided until we started talking. It isn't just that I don't want to be forced to leave my community. It isn't just that I might lose my husband. It's something more fundamental — who would I be with that identity stripped from me?"

"Free?" I ventured.

"It's a nice word," she said. "But who wants to be free like refugees are free? Like displaced persons are free? Like pariahs are free? That's a very cruel and hard freedom — if it's freedom at all."

I nodded.

"Whistle-blowers may be proud of what they've done," she said, "but are they ever happy?"

"That's an interesting question," I said. "Write about that."

She glanced at me. For the first time she looked interested.

"Tell me more," Sheila said.

"You're wondering if the risk is too great — and you've decided that it is. What if you held off on deciding that and learned more about the risk? What better way to learn about it than to interview some whistle-blowers and see how they fared? Would they do it again? Do they think it was worth it? Are any of them happy?"

"Interesting!" she exclaimed. "What I like about this idea," she said after a moment, "is that it's a lovely way to keep the question open. But it's more than that — I like it for what it is. The question interests me."

"Then let's consider that that's what you're going to be working on. First you'll have to see if that book's been done —"

"And if it has, I want to read it!"

"And even if it *has* been done, it may not have really addressed this thing that interests you — if a person can blow the whistle and find happiness afterward. You may find some books that come close to doing this job, but maybe don't really."

"That's my intuition," she said. "I have this hunch that the book I would do hasn't been done yet."

We talked for a while longer about the mechanics of her new project: what research she needed to do, what questions she might ask, what sorts of whistle-blowers made the most sense to interview. This was easy — so easy compared to the risk involved in exposing the secrets of her community! But just because it was easy didn't mean it wasn't the perfect place to begin. As part of her investigation as to whether or not she would make that other courageous journey, it was a reasonable first step.

You and Society

You might want to begin your exploration of your relationship to your culture and your society by answering the following questions:

- How does mass culture affect you?
- How do your affinity groups — your ethnic group, your religious group, your professional group — affect you?

- Which aspects of society affect you the most?
- For each one that you identify, ask yourself, "How *exactly* does it affect me?"
- What strategies might you employ to deal with all these cultural constraints?

Unless we are living alone in some rural wilderness, each of us is embedded in some culture and some society. That society is our safety net; it is our oppressor; it is our audience. It is no wonder that a creative person would find it hard, verging on impossible, to fashion a single, simple way of relating to society. However, your best life in the arts depends on your realizing that these realities exist. It also depends on your making decisions about what role you want to adopt vis-à-vis your culture, how you want to handle social and psychological self-censorship, and what you intend to do to tackle your feelings of alienation.

Appendix 1

YOUR ARTIST PLAN

Y ou are an artist — and you are also a project manager. You are obliged to create plans and schedules, to set goals, and to monitor the state of your creative projects, your creative career, and your creative life. Before we turn to an examination of you as project manager, let's summarize a bit. The following are seven key ideas that summarize the material we've been covering:

1. *Understand what you are up against.* Our personalities produce difficulties, the creative work we attempt produces difficulties, and the world we live in, which includes our society, our relationships, and the art marketplace, produces difficulties. Fully acknowledging the extent to which our life is a project beset by this array of difficulties and shadows, and that it will *always* be beset by this array of difficulties and shadows,

is better than hoping and pining for the facts of existence to be different. *You* are not easy, *writing* your novel is not easy, and *selling* your novel is not easy. So be it.

2. *Take your own side.* What will make this marathon race easier is being your own best friend, advocate, and advisor. This means creating strong intentions that meet your vision of how you want to live and how you want to make yourself proud, aligning your thoughts with those intentions and ridding yourself of thoughts that do not serve you, and aligning your behaviors with your intentions and ridding yourself of behaviors that do not align with your intentions. When you nominate yourself as the hero of your own story, you start to think and act like that hero.

3. *Show up.* What will also make this marathon race easier, in addition to your taking your own side, is showing up, not attaching to outcomes, and embracing the reality of process. You go into the dark and you do the work. You do not keep trying to turn on a light that does not exist, a light that will allow you to know before you know and that will prevent you from making mistakes and messes. You do not keep wishing and hoping that each thing you begin will turn out well. Each new day is a day to sit down, surrender, and do the work.

4. *Explore your anxieties and learn anxiety-management techniques.* Anxieties plague artists, and it is vital that you understand the role that anxiety plays in your life, where and how it manifests itself, and what you are going to do about it. Anxiety may be preventing you from learning difficult repertoire, from trying your hand at painting in a new idiom, from entering or doing well at competitions, from talking to agents, even from approaching the blank canvas or the blank

computer screen. Anxiety is your friend since it can accurately warn you of danger; it is your enemy since it can stir up your defenses for no good reason; and it is your lifelong partner.

5. *Practice some existential magic.* Get in the habit of creating new meaning in your life, of investing meaning in your current ideas and projects and in new ideas and projects, of starting each day in right relationship to meaning by announcing that you matter, that your efforts matter, and that you are going to seize meaning opportunities as they arise.

6. *Have a life.* Don't imagine that creating well or having a successful career in the arts is enough. You also need a life — or, to put it in meaning language, you need to make meaning in more ways than just via creating. Luckily, many additional meaning opportunities are available to you. That rich life might include relationships, a meaningful second career, activism, a disciplined practice of some sort in addition to your morning creativity practice, along with time-outs, relaxation, enjoyment, and "meaning-neutral" periods during which you don't pester yourself about meaning.

7. *Prove the exception.* Most people won't create regularly. Don't follow in their footsteps. Most people won't market their work energetically. Don't follow in their footsteps. Most people will avoid the darkness of not knowing and never go deep. Don't follow in their footsteps. Most people will never engage in the kind of personal analysis and self-awareness that I've been preaching, analysis that includes, for example, identifying what language doesn't serve you and changing it. Don't follow in their footsteps. Prove the exception!

Daily, Monthly, and Long-Range Planning

As a lifelong project manager, you are obliged to engage in daily, monthly, and long-range planning. Here are some tips to help with all three. Let's begin with eight straightforward elements of a daily plan:

1. Start each day with a simple, eloquent plan, such as "I am writing today."

2. Create a daily mantra that you use to keep yourself on track. It might be something like "I stay the course" or "Process" or "Effort, not outcome" or any other phrase that resonates for you.

3. Actively plan your day. Get a picture of when you're creating, how many creative stints you're penciling in, when you mean to do your art business, and so on. Plan your day to include both creating and the business of art.

4. First thing each day, take a moment to think through where you want to invest meaning, and then move effortlessly and without a fuss directly into your morning creativity practice.

5. Plan for anything else that you consider important, like an AA meeting, some cognitive work, or some anxiety-management work.

6. If you start to get down, remember to choose meaning over mood and to talk yourself back from doubts, worries, sadness, and all the rest. Try to keep yourself focused on the meaning you intend to make and not on the mood you find yourself in.

7. Be prepared to use small increments of time as they arise. Part of daily planning is remaining on your toes throughout the day so that you can deal with everyday emergencies and changed circumstances and use time

as it arises for additional creative stints and additional business efforts.

8. Go to bed mindfully, maybe by posing yourself a sleep-thinking prompt such as "I wonder what John and Mary want to chat about in chapter 2?" or "I wonder whom to approach with my new suite of paintings?" By going to bed this way, you ask your brain to continue working on your behalf and you set yourself up for a productive next morning.

Next, let's look at eight straightforward elements of a three-month plan (you can plan in a monthly way or you can plan in a three-monthly way; I think that choosing three months is a good idea):

1. *Create a system that allows you to keep track of three months at a time.* You might use a large white board, a software solution, or an old-fashioned paper planner.

2. *Identify weekly creative goals.* You'll be identifying daily goals as part of your daily planning; as part of your three-month planning, identify weekly goals like "complete a draft of chapter 2" or "start and finish one pumpkin painting."

3. *Identify weekly marketing goals.* This might sound like "contact two dozen literary agents with my email query" or "start the process of finding someone to build my website" or "search the net for London art galleries that might take an interest in my work."

4. *Create backward timelines from when things are due or from when things are needed, and pencil in the appropriate target goals.* For example, if your manuscript is due to your publisher in six months, create a backward timeline from that deadline and pencil in weekly goals that align with meeting that deadline.

5. *Pencil in special events, such as open studio weekends*

or gallery visits. Also pencil in the special risks you'd like to take, for instance, by choosing a particular day when you intend to cold-call that gallery owner you've had your eye on.

6. *Note your networking opportunities during the coming three months.* These might include the annual party that local publishers throw downtown, the openings of other artists' shows, the conference your romance writers' chapter is holding that agents and editors are attending, and so on.

7. *Pencil in the vacations you mean to take with your creative work* — the weekend in the country you're setting aside to plot your mystery, the day at the shore in the company of your sketchbook, and so on.

8. *Pencil in dates with your other loves.* If your novel is your primary creative project during this three-month period, but you also want to work on an art quilt and get a piece of wearable art made, you indicate on your calendar which Saturday you're devoting to the one and which weekend you're devoting to the other. In this way you get your main creative work done, but you also pay attention to your other interests.

Naturally you'll need to update this three-month picture as you go (which is one reason I like to use erasable boards). For example, if you happen not to meet a weekly goal, you simply forgive yourself and you recalibrate your goals for the remainder of the three months. In this way you know exactly what you're intending to accomplish each week and you keep yourself regularly updated.

Next, let's look at long-range planning. Here are eight things to keep in mind:

1. *Maintain a sensible balance between dreaming big dreams and testing those dreams in the crucible of*

reality. Part of your long-range planning should include some regular way of making sure that you still *have* dreams and some regular way of making sure that you are being *real* in your efforts to realize those dreams. If you decide to keep some sort of ongoing or long-range planner, you will want to regularly check in with yourself on the matter of dream-upholding and reality-testing.

2. *Include some regular way of reminding yourself that while creating is not the only meaning opportunity available to you, it is one of your most important ones.* Also remind yourself that if you're feeling low on meaning, creating is a great way to make some new meaning. If you decide to keep some sort of ongoing or long-range planner, you will want to regularly check in with yourself about how often you are using your ability to create as part of your meaning-making efforts.

3. *Keep track of how well or how poorly you're doing with the rhythm of starting creative projects, working on them, completing them, showing them, and selling them.* That is, you want to make sure that you are going through lots and lots of complete cycles with projects and not just starting them and abandoning them. If you decide to keep some sort of ongoing or long-range planner, you will want to regularly check in with yourself on how often you are finishing the things that you start.

4. *Keep track of how quickly or how slowly your body of work is growing.* Your goal, of course, is to make seamless transitions from creative project to creative project and to build a satisfying body of work over time. If you decide to keep some sort of ongoing or long-range planner, you will want to regularly check in with yourself to make sure that you are actively building a

body of work, which is one of the ways that we make ourselves proud.

5. *Keep track of your marketplace connections and of changes in the marketplace that affect you.* To take one example, you keep track of current self-publishing options and how the electronic delivery of books has changed the publishing landscape. If you decide to keep some sort of ongoing or long-range planner, you will want to regularly check in with yourself on whether your understanding of the marketplace is up-to-date enough.

6. *Regularly catch up with yourself and keep track of milestones, developmental changes, and whatever else is new in your life.* You aren't quite the same person after you've had a few gallery shows as you were before you had your first one; you aren't quite the same person after your novel has been rejected fifty times as you were before you began sending it out. Our life experiences matter — and it's hard to know *how* they matter unless we stop and check in with ourselves. If you decide to keep some sort of ongoing or long-range planner, you will want to regularly check in with yourself about who you now are and what matters to you.

7. *Keep track of how well you're dealing with the many challenges that we've been discussing, such as marketplace disappointments, losses of confidence, new stressors, and all the rest.* You want to keep sharp track so that you will be quick to notice if some challenge or another is getting the better of you. If you decide to keep some sort of ongoing or long-range planner, you will want to regularly check in with yourself about the challenges you face and about how exactly you intend to address them.

8. *Continue your cognitive work and maintain it in an ongoing way, noticing those thoughts that don't serve*

you, disputing those thoughts, and substituting more useful inner language. If you decide to keep some sort of ongoing or long-range planner, you will want to regularly check in with yourself on how well your self-talk is serving you.

The average youth finds planning and scheduling too boring for words. As we grow older, it dawns on us that creating a smart routine amounts to a real service that only we can provide for ourselves. Phrases such as *daily practice* take on a new, poignant meaning as we notice how much time we've lost by *not* planning and scheduling and by *not* keeping to our plans and schedules. Institute simple, sensible daily plans, monthly (or three-monthly) plans, and long-range plans. You're unlikely to achieve your best life in the arts without them.

Envisioning the Coming Twelve Months

Use the following tips for getting a handle on your next twelve months:

1. Pick a distant target date for the completion of a big project — say, Mother's Day for the completion of your suite of flower paintings. In your mind's eye, slowly move through the calendar year toward your target date, experiencing the generous amount of time at your disposal between the present moment and your completion date.
2. Get seven decks of cards and lay them all out on your living room rug. The cards in front of you amount to a year's worth of days, give or take a few. Let the magnitude of this sink in. Experience the wonderful availability of time.
3. Do a little simultaneous picturing. Picture you creating in your work space. Simultaneously experience

the fullness of a year. Connect these two rich feelings into one feeling of abundance.

4. Picture in your mind's eye the amount of creative work you'd like to accomplish in the coming year, mentally calculate how much time that allows for each project, and then write out your goals for the whole year on a one-year calendar.

5. Carefully count the number of days separating two holidays — for instance, the number of days separating New Year's Day and the Fourth of July — and envision starting a large project on that first holiday and completing it by the second.

6. Picture a single month in your mind's eye. You might picture the calendar page for January, say, and mentally pencil in a slew of creating days. Be optimistic, and fill that month with your creative efforts; and then in your mind's eye move on to February, then March, and so on.

7. Create a backward timeline, or several backward timelines, from important dates in the coming year, like the two gallery shows that you know about, the delivery date of your nonfiction manuscript, deadlines for grants and residencies, and so on.

8. Create a backward timeline, or several backward timelines, from important goals that you intend to set for yourself in the coming twelve months. Say that you decide you want to have six new sculptures done by June 1, before you leave for your annual vacation. Figure out how much time that allows for each one, and transfer that information to your three-month calendar.

9. Think through the contours of the year. Are you busy teaching for three months and then freer to create during the two months thereafter? Calculate in your mind's eye how much work you'll tackle in those busy

months and how much more work you'll tackle in those freer months.

10. Create an actual, full-year, oversize calendar, maybe made up of twelve large sheets of paper that fill a whole wall. On those big sheets you would mark workshop dates, conference dates, contest deadlines, and so on, as well as your creative goals. You might use this instead of your three-month calendar or in addition to it — using it in addition is not overkill, since you really can't have too much organization!

You have a human-size chance to create a subjectively rich and objectively successful life in the arts. You better your odds by thoughtfully considering the issues I've presented and by making a concerted effort to arrive at your personalized conclusions and solutions. It is really unlikely that your best life in the arts will just happen. Yes, luck is a factor; yes, there's no accounting for the gods of whimsy. But I hope that you now know what *you* need to do. There's nothing left to do but to wish you the best of luck!

REFRESHER COURSE OF NINETY-SEVEN CREATIVITY TIPS

We've covered a lot of ground! I'd like to present some tips that summarize our discussion, tips you can dip into whenever you need a refresher course. Please enjoy!

1. Be consistent in showing up. Getting to your creative work only once in a while won't keep it alive. Make *routine* and *regularity* sacred words!

2. Who knows how many artists fail because the light that shines through them is refracted in a thousand directions and not concentrated in a single beam? Pick projects and complete them! It is not really possible to work on a thousand things at once.

3. One of the best ways to help yourself create every day is to craft a starting ritual that you begin to use regularly and routinely. When your ritual becomes habitual you will find yourself moving effortlessly from not creating to creating.

4. Make the following pledge: "I will do some creative work every day, if only for fifteen or twenty minutes." Honor your pledge for the next two weeks, and spend fourteen consecutive days creating.

5. Are you looking for the perfect time to create? Forget about it! You are always in the middle of something, so it is right in the middle of things that your creating also must happen.

6. Even small amounts of time can be used for creating. Do you make use of fifteen minutes here and twenty minutes there?

7. Are you good at capturing your creative thoughts? Or do you let them slip away by telling yourself that they weren't really all that good or all that important? Stop that! Start right now doing a better job of capturing and recording your ideas.

8. You must reckon with your own character. Creativity requires curiosity. Are you curious enough? Creativity requires risk-taking. Are you willing to risk? Creativity requires energy. Can you marshal and unleash your energy? Creativity requires patience. Have you cultivated that quality? Turn yourself into the artist you need to be!

9. Telling our truth can bring us pain and get us into trouble, but worse pain and worse trouble await us if we keep silent. Tell your truth — carefully, artfully, and courageously!

10. Say yes to your creative work! Avoid *maybe* like the plague. Maybe is a state that takes you right to the edge of meaninglessness. Maybe plays to your weaknesses, your anxieties, and your doubts. Maybe frustrates and disappoints you. Avoid the maybe trap!

11. Reframe *discipline* as *devotion*. Luciano Pavarotti said, "People think I'm disciplined. It's not discipline, it's

devotion, and there's a great difference." Think about that difference!

12. Boredom is the thing that regularly arrives between excitements and episodes of meaning. If you are bored do not say, "I am so bored that I can't possibly create." Instead say, "I am so bored — I had better create!"

13. Have you figured out a form for your creative work? Nothing really exists until it has a form!

14. What's your process, your style, and your rhythm? Get clear in your own mind how you create. Then accept your way of working — or change it if it's not effective.

15. To decide to reach for this blue and not that one; to switch styles or subject matter; to move, in the middle of a sentence, in one direction or another; and to commit to this book when that one is also calling — these are the sorts of choices that artists must make if they are to function. Remember: you can't avoid choosing!

16. You can jump-start your creativity in the following way: 1) Ask yourself an interesting question. 2) Try to answer it.

17. Unexplored territory has no maps. You will have to go into the unknown guided only by your inner compass. Become an intrepid explorer!

18. Wildness is part of the process. Say, "I am one wild creature!" Shout it out, if you dare!

19. Do not fear the darkness. It is in that darkness that your new work resides. You must proceed blind and uncertain into that darkness if you intend to go deep. Down in that darkness reside your future accomplishments.

20. Not everything you create will work well. When something doesn't work you can say, "I'm an idiot!" or you can say, "Such things happen." Which thought do you suppose serves you better?

21. Creativity flows from self-relationship. You are the student and you are the teacher. The next time a creative

problem arises, ask yourself, "What do I already know that will help me solve this?" Begin to see yourself as your own best resource.

22. Allow for fortunate accidents. Figuratively pull out odds and ends from your refrigerator. Try combinations of food — pickles with peanut butter, apple juice with radish slices. Most will taste horrible. But maybe one will be a revelation!

23. Intending is more powerful than wishing. Intend to create. Hold the intention in your heart and in your belly. Grow creative through *powerful intention*.

24. How satisfactory is your life between your creative stints? Are there some important improvements to be made? As much as we might wish it to be, life isn't only about creating!

25. Creativity is your teacher. Pick a creative project whose express purpose is to teach you something about your situation or your nature. If no project comes to mind, try your hand at a ten-page autobiography.

26. Have you abandoned some creative project that still retains a lot of juice? Return to it with optimism, an open heart, and a firm belief in renewed possibility!

27. If you regularly block, what do you think are the sources of your blockage? Do you block only on certain work? Do you block at certain points in the process? Do you block at certain times of the year? Become your own expert on blockage!

28. Learn some anxiety-management techniques. Anxiety makes us undisciplined. Learn a deep-breathing technique or a relaxation technique to help you stay put. Anxiety is part of the process — learn how to manage it!

29. A creative block is the wall you erect to ward off the anxiety you suppose you'll experience if you sit down to work. Don't predict that anxiety! And if it happens to come — so what? You can manage your anxiety.

30. Time magically disappears, but it appears only when you schedule it. Put creating on your schedule!

31. You can't plan in advance for everything — for every mood swing, every mistake, and every shift in your circumstances. But you can plan to show up — that is three-quarters of the battle!

32. Learn how to go directly to your work. When your work bell tolls at the appointed hour, answer it. Stop waiting!

33. To repeat: schedule your creativity. Prepare a schedule for getting to your creative projects and commit to that schedule. Work on your current project for a month without second-guessing your choice or bad-mouthing your progress.

34. Create first thing each morning. An hour of creating before your "real day" begins prevents a day of guilty feelings. Start each day making some meaning. Grow creative by putting creating first!

35. Work every day on a creative project, even for just an hour, Saturdays and Sundays included.

36. Don't shrug away the fact that you're not completing your creative work. Get to the last sentence of the last page of the last revision. Then launch your piece into the marketplace. If you are not completing projects, do not accept that from yourself!

37. Divide a sheet of paper into three columns. Label the first column "Starting," the second column "Working," and the third column "Completing." List as many strategies as you can to help you start, work, and complete your creative projects.

38. Creativity at times needs solitude. If solitude is eluding you, find an empty room right now, and do not leave it for two or three hours. Go to a quiet place and work!

39. What do you need to unlearn in order to become more creative?

40. Enjoy the process — the mistakes and messes along with the successes. Don't need for your work to go smoothly. The ups and downs are part of the process.

41. Get cognitively stronger! Use the following three-step cognitive technique: 1) Identify negative thoughts like "I have no talent." 2) Dispute them by saying, "No, that's not true!" 3) Replace them with affirmations like "Of course I'm talented!" Start today to get a better grip on your mind.

42. You might recognize that *talent* is so loaded a word that you would be wise to forget about it altogether and just keep on working. Forget about talent. Concentrate on showing up.

43. Grow creative by not fearing mistakes. Make a mess of a watercolor. Make a hash of a sonnet. Feel the feelings that come with making stupid mistakes. Then say, "I can survive these feelings!" Remind yourself that you must grow very easy with mistakes and messes.

44. Affirm your creative efforts. Affirmations are not bound up in rules. An affirmation can be long or short, poetic or plain. If you love a phrase and find that it helps you, then it is a valid affirmation. Create some powerful affirmations!

45. Who isn't a little inclined to take shortcuts? But be careful! Shortcuts can kill the creative process. Avoid illegitimate shortcuts when creating.

46. Self-deception stifles creativity. Anatole France put it this way: "It is in the ability to deceive oneself that the greatest talent is shown." Are there any truths that you need to admit to yourself? Admit them!

47. Art happens on dull days too. Do not wait for inspiration. Do not wait for anything. Grow creative by regularly and routinely creating.

48. We have enough experiences in a day to make art for a decade. Never fear a shortage of great ideas. If you show up often enough and grow quiet enough to hear them, great ideas will percolate right up.

49. Make sure you have a private space where you can get your creative work done. Make that space. Secure that space. Get agreements so that no one will bother you in your space. Create, secure, and honor your space!

50. If you live with people — with parents, with a mate, with children, with roommates — get agreements. Let them know that often in your private space, silence is golden, and that sometimes you are not available.

51. Say to yourself, "What does my creative work require?" and honor your answer. Need to tidy up your space? Get some supplies? Do some research? Do it!

52. Many people are embarrassed to create in public. It feels unseemly to them, like kissing in plain view. Deal with that self-consciousness! Learn to make a spectacle of yourself. If you don't, you'll feel uncreative everywhere except in your private space.

53. Feeling too chaotic to create? Don't think that way! Instead say, "Let me take this chaos and use it to create a world." Invite that unwanted guest right into your private space.

54. Revere beauty without becoming enchanted by it. Aim for it but also aim for truth and goodness, just in case they, and not beauty, are the real things of value.

55. Concentrate, but also surrender. Surrender, but also concentrate. Sometimes the one, sometimes the other, always both!

56. Creativity requires persistence. Are you practiced at sticking to things for years at a time?

57. Learn by doing. There is no other way. Experience is the best and only real teacher. Grow creative through conscious effort!

58. As you shop your creative projects you'll find yourself waiting on news from the marketplace. While you're waiting, be patient but not idle. Responses from the world can take a very long time! Keep working.

59. Mystery is the artist's territory. Excellence lies in the direction of mystery! Let go of your need to know and buy bewilderment instead.

60. It is remarkable that we can hold the entirety of a year in our imaginations long enough to make decisions about what we'd like to accomplish. Practice this useful skill right now. Picture the coming year and make decisions about what you want to start, work on, and complete.

61. Know your own rhythms. During what part of the year do you generate the most ideas? When do you need to rest? When do you like to play? Honor your unique process by making room on your calendar for your needs.

62. Expect setbacks. No artist experiences one success after another. Determine to come back. Remember that you will need to demonstrate your courage all over again.

63. There's necessary arrogance and unnecessary arrogance. Learn the difference. Your creative life depends on fostering the one and minimizing the other.

64. There are just too many ideas to keep in one's head. Coax yourself into the habit of organization. Get better organized, and stay organized.

65. What if it takes years and years to create beautifully or to sell anything? You will need stamina. To repeat: creativity requires persistence. Get fit and stay fit — emotionally as well as physically.

66. When we aren't really using ourselves, we feel disappointed and depressed. Use yourself! Challenge

yourself more, take new risks, inaugurate grand projects, and use yourself to full capacity.

67. There is always the doing — the repeated doing over time — by which we learn our craft. Do so much that you become a master, even as you remain your own apprentice.

68. Do you have a plan to survive the countless rejections that will come your way? Create that plan!

69. Do you keep your creative work close enough? Is it always available? Keep it so close that when you turn around you run right into it!

70. It is so much more exhausting not to work than to work. If you procrastinate you'll feel more exhausted than if you'd created for hours. Never forget how tired not working makes you feel.

71. If you love solitude and indwelling, you can live much too claustrophobically. Remember to throw open your windows and let some fresh air in!

72. Whatever pain and suffering you've experienced has been a blessing at least in this regard: you know some true things that you couldn't have learned any other way. Do those experiences find a way into your art?

73. Do you need creating to be easy? If you do, change your mind! Creating is often exhausting. Accept that you've embarked on an arduous journey.

74. You and you alone decide what is meaningful. Use your creative nature to make new meaning each day. Treat meaning as a wellspring and a renewable resource, and you will never run short of meaning again.

75. Take that risky first step. Picture yourself separated from your creative work by a chasm that is a thousand feet deep but only a foot wide. Yes, it is deep! But see how easy it is to cross right over?

76. Create everywhere. Create in the rain. Create by the side of the road. Create wherever you find yourself!

77. Say, "I will astonish myself." Then you're bound to astonish others.

78. You are an individual. Think for yourself. Decide for yourself. Create in your own voice!

79. Don't say that you're unable to craft beautiful things until you've given yourself years and years of trying. What if your grand piece is destined to be your ninth and you stop at eight?

80. Forget about control. We are in control of so little! Aim for influence instead. Become a positive influence on your creative life.

81. Set grand goals and mean them. It is better to have a grand goal and really work toward it than to half-set a paltry goal and, because of its paltriness, find that you're bored even before you've started.

82. Often you're resistant to getting started. That resistance is just a thin veneer between you and your work, but it feels like a concrete wall. Get up and crash right through it! Feel like a bull or a battering ram. Don't let a film of resistance cost you decades.

83. Creating involves you in an endless series of decisions: this project must be abandoned, this project must *not* be abandoned, this project is gorgeous but will earn you nothing, this project is mediocre but marketable. No one can make these decisions but you.

84. There may be days when the work frustrates you horribly. Maybe you'll downright hate it. Those are the days to love your work! Remember to love your work especially on the days when you hate it.

85. If you hide your work away, no one can criticize or reject it. Isn't that clever! But does that foolproof protective maneuver really serve you?

86. You must appraise your work. Appraising isn't cold-hearted criticism. It is the effort you make to turn

your raw ideas into elaborated beauty. Appraising is your duty.

87. When there's no desire, there's no creativity. Fall in love with each of your creative projects! Burn to create.

88. You will never retire from creating. Why would you? Happily rush on, restlessly and hungrily, to the very end!

89. When a thing is not done, continuing to work on it is the strength. When it is done, the strength lies in stopping. Work, appraise, complete; work, appraise, complete: this is the creative life.

90. You *will* have your critics. What will you do about them?

91. Survival issues are bound to intrude. There is always the rent to pay. The facts of existence weigh heavily. Create anyway. It is the way we rejoice right in the middle of a hard reality!

92. Hope comes and goes. Sometimes it leaves for years and decades. Only you can rekindle your hope. Announce some new hope for your creative life, and take action in that direction.

93. There is no substitute for showing up. Really.

94. Invest in your current project. Do it and complete it. Then detach from it as you send it out into the world. Then invest in your next project. That is the dance: one of attachment and detachment.

95. Which parts of the process do you want to skip? The plotting? The cobbling? The revising? Learn which parts you are inclined to skip — and don't skip them!

96. In your mind's eye, picture yourself never giving up. If you are a writer, picture yourself still writing at thirty, at forty, at fifty, at sixty, at seventy, at eighty, at ninety, at a hundred. Picture yourself never giving up, despite the challenges that come your way.

97. Regularly congratulate yourself as you create — not out of narcissism but in your role as your own good friend and advocate. Be your own best supporter!

INDEX

criticism, 9–10, 215
culture, 47, 190–91
curiosity, 38, 206
customers, 106
    See also marketplace players

D

daily planning, 196–97
darkness, 207
days off, 77, 198
decisions, 214
defensiveness, 2, 10–11
demands, 83–85, 87
    of life, 102
    and opportunity, 90
dependency, 88
desire, 46, 58, 215
    See also passion
detachment, 215
devotion, 46, 206–7
disappointments, 200
discharge techniques, 96
discipline, 46, 206–7
disidentification, 38
dislikes, 33–34
distractions, 7–8
distress, 84
doing, 213
doubt, 11, 26, 31–32, 166

E

economic stress, 87–88
empathy, 103–27
    and marketplace players,
      115–19
    and preserving art
      relationships, 110–15
    and self-consciousness, 123–26
    simple, 126–27

energy, 38, 206
    mental, 44, 47–48
    motivational, 43
engagement, 183–90
en plein air painting, 123–26
enthusiasm, 38, 47, 106
ethics, 105, 183
eustress, 84
events, 70
exceptions, 67–71, 195
excitement, 38
exercise, 91
exhaustion, 46–47, 213
existential stress, 89
experience, 211

F

fatigue, mental, 8–9, 44
fears, 34
feelings, 9–14
fight-or-flight reflex, 93
finances, 181
finishing (work), 26, 49, 205, 209
focus, 8
Focused Journal Method, 136–42
follow-through, 69
form, 207
France, Anatole, 210
freedom, 63–82
    and anxiety, 82
    to be imperfect, 74–75
    fleeing from, 66
    internal, xiii
    to make meaning, 71–73
    to prove the exception, 67–71
    types of, 64–65
    ways artists give away, 75–81
    wondering about, 82
friendships, 28

O

obsessions, 14–18, 44–45, 76
openness, 25
opportunities, 76–77, 84, 87, 90, 134, 156–57, 195
organization, 27, 212

P

pain, 213
painting en plein air, 123–26
passion, 43–62
    appetite and addiction, 52–57
    and creation, 57–62
    cultural and societal
        injunctions against, 47
    negative, 54
    pursuit of, 62
    rekindling, 44–48, 58
    revisiting earliest, 51
    and voice, 48–52
patience, 206
Pavarotti, Luciano, 46, 206
perfection, 74–75
persistence, 77, 211, 212
personality, 130
physical stress, 89
picturing, simultaneous, 201–2
planning, 196–201
positioning, 49–50
possibilities, 34
principles, 159
procrastination, 213
progress, 49
progressive relaxation, 90
promotion, self-, 70–71
psychological freedom, 64–65
psychological stress, 89–90
psychosynthesis, 38
publicity, 70
public persona, 162–68

Q

questions, 132–33, 134–35, 207

R

Raeburn, Susan, 52
reaching out, 69, 76–77
reading people, 119–23
"real" self, 159–60
reciprocity, 94
recovery programs, 52, 53, 97
rejections, 213
relating, 109
relationships, 129–49, 169
    art of, 148–49
    and empathy, 110–15
    preserving, 112–15
    with self, 135–48, 207–8
    with society, 190–91
    stress, 88
    using personal to support art
        intentions, 134
Relaxation Response, 90–91
resistance, 26, 214
Rethinking Depression (Maisel), 71
rhythms, 212
risk, 35, 49, 53, 61, 65, 198, 206, 213
rituals, 95, 205

S

Sartre, Jean-Paul, 183
saying no, 29–30, 77
scheduling, 209
self-appraisal, 214–15
self-censorship, 65, 82, 171–74
self-consciousness, 123–26, 211
self-deception, 210
self-doubt, 31–32, 166
self-identifications, 151–53, 159–62
self-inquiry, 138

ABOUT THE AUTHOR

Eric Maisel, PhD, is the author of more than forty works of nonfiction and fiction and is widely regarded as America's foremost creativity coach. He trains creativity coaches nationally and internationally and provides core trainings for the Creativity Coaching Association. Eric is a print columnist for *Professional Artist* magazine and a blogger for *Fine Art America* and *Psychology Today*. In 2012 he developed natural psychology, the new psychology of meaning. His books include *Coaching the Artist Within*, *Rethinking Depression*, *Fearless Creating*, *The Van Gogh Blues*, and many others. He lives in the San Francisco Bay Area with his family.

His websites are www.ericmaisel.com and
www.naturalpsychology.net.

NEW WORLD LIBRARY is dedicated to publishing books and other media that inspire and challenge us to improve the quality of our lives and the world.

We are a socially and environmentally aware company, and we strive to embody the ideals presented in our publications. We recognize that we have an ethical responsibility to our customers, our staff members, and our planet.

We serve our customers by creating the finest publications possible on personal growth, creativity, spirituality, wellness, and other areas of emerging importance. We serve New World Library employees with generous benefits, significant profit sharing, and constant encouragement to pursue their most expansive dreams.

As a member of the Green Press Initiative, we print an increasing number of books with soy-based ink on 100 percent postconsumer-waste recycled paper. Also, we power our offices with solar energy and contribute to nonprofit organizations working to make the world a better place for us all.

Our products are available
in bookstores everywhere.
For our catalog, please contact:

New World Library
14 Pamaron Way
Novato, California 94949

Phone: 415-884-2100 or 800-972-6657
Catalog requests: Ext. 50
Orders: Ext. 52
Fax: 415-884-2199
Email: escort@newworldlibrary.com

To subscribe to our electronic newsletter, visit:
www.newworldlibrary.com